When Less Was More

Memories of a Sustainable Lifestyle

EDITED BY DAVOUD TEHRANI
AND RUTH WANGERIN

ISBN: 978-1-7334329-2-4 (Paperback)
ISBN: 978-1-7334329-1-7 (Ebook)

Library of Congress Control Number: 2019912824

Cover photo (Chefchaouen 37) by Fred Murphy
fredmurphyphotography.com

Cover design by Cal Sharp

Printed and bound in the United States of America
First edition

DAY Publishing
New York, NY
DAYpublishing.books@gmail.com

For our great, great, great, great, great grandchildren

TABLE OF CONTENTS

PREFACE

The past is brought back in this book as people of the older generations share stories about the sustainable life styles they used to live. These stories reveal a global experience, from as near as Brooklyn and as far as China, from Italy, Ghana, Kazakhstan, and France to Ecuador and the Dominican Republic. Thanks to the ethnic diversity of the New York metropolitan region, our students (at the College of Staten Island and Westchester Community College) were able to collect stories from all over the world simply by interviewing their own family elders and friends.

The idea started with casual conversations remembering our own childhoods. When Davoud described growing up in Iran, Ruth compared his experience with her own childhood. When Davoud created an interview outline for his own research in Iran, Ruth told him about the interview assignment she always included in her classes. When together we used the interview outline to interview Davoud's older sister Fatemeh in Tehran, and then two of her sons, we were both hooked. After that, Davoud continued to interview one person after another in various parts of Iran. Then, starting around 2010, we both gave this assignment to our classes in the New York metropolitan area over a period of several years.

The purpose of initiating this project with our students was to help the younger generation, who have known only the world of abundance, learn that it is indeed possible to satisfy one's needs without constant and excessive consumption. In these stories, parents and grandparents from all over the world are showing their children and grandchildren a better way to find happiness, through life in a community.

The interview assignment was always deeply appreciated by both the students and the elders whom they interviewed. All of the students who fulfilled this assignment learned a lot about sustainability and began to see that the mass consumption that shaped their lifestyles was not the only way to live. Most of the interviews presented in this anthology focused on the issue of sustainability and represent the widespread environmentalism among today's youth.

The people interviewed for these papers were from both rural and urban environments and from a variety of class backgrounds and occupations. It was striking to note how little difference informants remembered in the patterns of consumption between the poorer and more prosperous classes during their childhoods.

It was incredibly moving to read about the relationships our students had with their elders, to see their eyes opening to another time, and to hear so many of them state that another world is possible.

This is a selection from among the best of the student interviews, edited for length and readability. The interviews report rich details from the lives of elders and contemplate what really matters. These are not grandparents' stories of their pursuit of "the American dream" measured in money. Nor are these "rags-to-riches" narratives based on the American "foundational myth" of the "self-made man."[1] These are conversations between young and old on the question, "What is a good life?"

One striking finding of this project was that many college students (and some of their elders) associated a sustainable lifestyle with poverty. Of course, many residents of the rich nations treasure the comforts and instant gratifications provided by an economy based on mass production and mass consumption. The best interviews went beyond the simple question of whether the past was better or the future, whether the old country was better or America. The best papers critically examined the mental association of repairs and hand-me-downs with deprivation and of profligate waste with success. Students who were successful in this exercise moved beyond celebrating their ability to throw things away thanks to the hard work of their grandparents and instead began to pay attention to what their grandparents were telling them about valuing everything you have. In the most meaningful dialogues, students realized that the purpose of their grandparents' lives was not simply that they, the first person in the family to attend college, would have a closet full of clothes.

Through these wonderful dialogues, we hope some of the understanding of these elders will find its way into the next generation's understanding of how to both live "the good life" and also maintain, share, and pass along this beautiful world.

Davoud Tehrani and Ruth Wangerin, New York City

August, 2019

---

[1] Paul, H. (2014). Introduction. In *The Myths That Made America: An Introduction to American Studies* (pp. 11-42). Bielefeld: Transcript Verlag.

ACKNOWLEDGEMENTS

We are grateful to the people who shared their memories in these conversations and to the students whose reports of those dialogs appear in this anthology. The many undergraduates who sought out elders to interview and then discussed the results in class contributed to the project, whether or not their work ended up in this book. Thanks are also due to the Sociology and Anthropology Departments at the College of Staten Island and Westchester Community College for their support.

Because we live and work in New York City, it is only appropriate that we acknowledge that we are on traditional Lenape land that was taken by European migrants beginning in the 1600s. Today, we are privileged to join indigenous people in attempting to be good stewards of the land and to pass on Turtle Island (North America) and the whole beautiful globe in healthy condition to the seventh generation.

On a more personal level, we've been inspired by young environmentalists in the family, particularly Jenny and Eduardo, Arezu, Yousef, Mina, and Shoshana. Shirley Frank provided an editing boost (and kind words) when the task of working with so many student essays seemed daunting. Many friends, colleagues, and loved ones have helped us over the years to keep our priorities straight, and no list would be long enough to name them all; know that your spirits are alive.

Finally, we are grateful to the multitude of scientists, researchers, scholars, game wardens, park rangers, inventors, organic farmers, labor organizers, and social and environmental activists who have been working steadfastly to help humanity address the economic and environmental crises of our time.

When Less Was More

INTRODUCTION

The goal of this book is to share knowledge about the relatively
sustainable ways of life that were practiced all over the world
just one or two generations ago. The descriptions of these
lifestyles and the experiences of earlier generations are eye-
opening, especially to young people who, though they may
already be involved in environmental movements, are familiar
only with today's culture of individualism, mass production
and mass consumption.

The interview project

College students were assigned to interview an elder about
details of daily life in the recent past. Most students
interviewed their grandparents or other older relatives. The
cross-generational dialogue was enjoyable to both old and
young, as can be seen in the selections that follow. But equally
important, what students—including those whose full reports
are not included in this anthology—learned affected their own
thinking about how to live.

Students were surprised to learn how much consumption
patterns in the older generation were different from their own
patterns, and that these differences were not necessarily

related to income levels. Both poor and middle-class people limited consumption. Hand-me-downs were a general practice. An 82-year-old grandfather from Sicily said, regarding clothing, "we had more with less." A 90-year-old woman, originally from River Road, Grenada, told her great granddaughter,

> I didn't know I was poor until I got older. To be honest, I still don't think I was poor because I enjoyed my life. And I never felt like I didn't have what I needed to survive. So, to this day I still don't think I was poor.

One of the issues most of the elders complained about was the amount of waste in today's lifestyle, and many of the students added their own experiences. One student who worked in a prestigious Manhattan bakery was aghast at the wastefulness and disrespect of the bakery's practice of throwing away any unsold unpackaged food at the end of the day. Another student wrote,

> I've witnessed people spending their whole check on outfits and shoes in order to impress and appear as if they have the best clothes. They would go without food and risk getting evicted all to be "fashion" forward.

Students were surprised, impressed, and envious to learn that their parents or grandparents had spent a lot of time outdoors and unsupervised when they were children. We, the editors, could have told them that, of course; it's concerned us over the years to meet so many students who have little sense of where food comes from, can't name the plants in the neighborhood, and don't know north from south.

After talking with their parents and grandparents, students commented that American children born in the last few decades spend more time indoors than outdoors and are often alone. The interviews led to discussions in class about how today's children are separated early from the natural environment and do not discover for themselves the scientific realities of this planet. Rather than playing with dirt, they learn to fear it. Rather than meeting all the neighborhood kids and exploring their surroundings together, they are forbidden to venture beyond the house and backyard or to meet other children except in supervised activities. The weather becomes something to complain about. The sunrise and sunset have little practical significance.

Animals are a part of nature and of our subsistence system that are virtually inaccessible to children growing up in cities, who tend to think of animals as pets, characters in children's books, or captives in zoos. Contrast the inexperience of today's city kids with animals to the memories of a grandmother from Ecuador:

> Back when I was a child I played with the domestic animals we had in the farm. It was so much fun, and I believe other children loved doing the same. Children were more attached to nature, which was great because they grew with the mentality that they had to take care of their environment.

Many young people use the term "technology" to refer only to recent electronic devices such as smart phones, with the implication that no technology of importance existed before they were born. Thus it was instructive to them to learn about clever technologies used in the past, perhaps for thousands of years, which not only did a necessary job but did it effectively and sustainably.

For example, yesteryear's cooling and heating systems might seem inefficient compared to high-tech systems of today, but they were much more sustainable. Through the memories of older people, we and the students (re)discovered ingenious time-proven, natural systems for using rain water, preserving foods, and keeping warm in the winter and cool in the summer.

Children's toys and games were among the favorite subjects explored in many of the interviews. Students were aware that nowadays unused – often expensive – toys clutter the homes of families with children. So they were surprised to learn that hardly anyone ever bought toys until quite recently. Even more exciting was their discovery that their own grandparents, who claim to have no interest in cellphones or computers, were astonishingly inventive in their youth.

Whether or not their family had cash to spare, most people older than 50 or 60 today remember a time when almost all toys were homemade, often by the children themselves. Play was both creative and sustainable. While some types of play were typical of a specific local environment, like a farm, certain toys seem to have been found on all sides of the oceans. Children everywhere pretended to "drive" the furniture, used empty cans and a wire or string to make a "telephone," and banged on pans or whatever they could find to imitate the sound of drums.

Games in which kids imitate adults were also common. Everywhere children played "shop." A Jamaican grandmother remembered that they used to gather leaves from a breadfruit tree and set up a pretend tropical shop with groceries from the market.

In these conversations, students sometimes asked people who had lived "back in the day" what they thought about the way that people live now. One grandmother replied that she finds the current times very stressful – you need a lot of money to survive and it's hard to raise children, she said. When she was younger, there were clearer values and people spent much more time with their families. The way of life was more or less the same for all families, and that reduced stress and competition.

Many aspects of this community-oriented, low-waste lifestyle are still being practiced, in families, in community organizations, in neighborhoods, and in rural districts. For example, in traditional western Catskill rural areas it is not unusual to see roadside vegetable stands based on the honor system, with a sign listing the prices and a cup or slot to place the money.

HONOR SYSTEM, DELAWARE COUNTY, NEW YORK: TAKE A PUMPKIN AND LEAVE YOUR MONEY IN THE LUNCHBOX

Methodology

The interviews included in this book were the work of students in several different classes over several semesters, in several different subjects, at two different colleges, taught by two different professors with somewhat different approaches. For each professor, the assignment also evolved over those semesters.

To introduce the assignment, both professors handed out a short essay by Dr. Tehrani about environmental issues and the need for humanity to move toward a more sustainable lifestyle. The essay, a revised version of which is reproduced in the Appendix, discussed mass production and mass consumption, the proliferation of waste, and basic information about the climate crisis and depletion/ destruction of resources. Students were provided with a suggested "interview schedule," below, a list of questions to guide them in their interviews. Included in the instructions were examples of the kinds of answers some of Dr. Tehrani's interviewees in Iran had given to these questions, such as ingenious toys they used to make for themselves. The examples stimulated the students' imaginations and helped them seek similarly fascinating details from their own elders.

Many of Dr. Tehrani's sociology students completed the entire interview schedule and discussed environmental issues at length in their papers. Dr. Wangerin's social research and cultural anthropology students approached the project somewhat differently. Human adaptation to the environment was a theme of the course, especially in cultural anthropology, so this interview was one step in exploring that theme while it was also an exercise in research methodology. Dr. Wangerin's students, especially in the later semesters, were assigned to conduct a "life history" project that was organized as an intergenerational dialogue focused on issues of sustainability. They were urged to concentrate the interview on the topics that most interested their elders and that resulted in the most thought-provoking dialogue. Dr. Wangerin required students to follow a set format in writing up the interview experience, including the setting and other personal touches.

Dr. Tehrani conducted over a dozen interviews himself with old-timers in various regions of Iran. The selections based on these interviews do not (with the exception of the first) exude the same feeling of family intimacy as some of the students' interviews. However, they are rich in details about traditional sustainable technologies. Taken together, the interviews from Iran, the USA, and countries from around the globe illustrate that many sustainable practices, such as minimal consumption, were the most prevalent lifestyle around the globe until quite recently.

Interview schedule

The following are the interview topics and questions given to students (without the explanations inom the original handout):
1. Consumption patterns (e.g., how many pairs of shoes, what happened to clothes once outgrown)
2. Cooling and heating systems
3. Means of transportation
4. Waste (e.g., how much garbage, what was thrown away)
5. Children's activities and toys
6. Leisure time
7. Climate change and the environment (e.g., could they see the stars at night, could they drink from the rivers)
8. Comparing the old and the new
9. Community life

We hope the readers of this anthology will agree that many of the students made more of this assignment than we had dared to hope.

PART ONE: UNITED STATES

Back in the Old Days

Paula Benyei

KINGSTON, NY

I interviewed Rose Woods, an amazingly fit 86-year-old retired RN who's been volunteering at Kingston Hospital two days a week, like clockwork, since her mandatory retirement at age seventy and one-half in 2000. She doesn't "hear so good" anymore, but her mind is still sharp. She was born in the first weeks of 1929 to a Polish immigrant couple, "somewhere around the middle" of a brood of five girls and three boys. Little did the family know the Great Depression was right around the corner.

Most of Rosie's childhood was defined not only by her parents' unskilled, poor (very poor) Catholic immigrant status, but made worse by the greatest period of financial difficulty in our nation's history, which limited any opportunity for upward mobility. Luckily this would end just in time for their children, Rosie included, to get out on their own. By the time the economy recovered enough to see opportunities ahead, Rose was grown up and planning to marry her sweetheart just home from WWII.

Rosie's family grew up in a section of Kingston, NY, derisively known as "Polack Alley" – a term to which she seems to take no offense – where she still lives. Of the eight children, six spent their entire lives living and working in Kingston, four of them within walking distance of their childhood home.

Polish was the primary language spoken and Roman Catholicism the religion. The children all attended a Catholic school (in an old Victorian home donated to the nuns), where classes were all taught in Polish and the masses, attended at least three days a week, were also in Polish exclusively.

While they considered their neighborhood to be "'in the city," most families lived on 2-5 acre lots. The houses all lined up shoulder to shoulder at the curb on very long and narrow plots with surprisingly large yards in back. Most of this space was devoted to livestock and fruit trees and to vegetables planted March to November on every available inch of soil.

When I asked if she ever took vacations with the family, Rosie looked at me as if I were nuts. "No, we were poor, but it was like a vacation every day." Which will seem both an outrageous overstatement and a fantastic testament to a happy childhood when I tell you her story. In fact, speaking of vacations, another family that lived in New York City used to come stay with them for the summer. Two more children showed up on the last day of school in June and stayed until Labor Day, their parents coming up on weekends and returning to work during the week to escape the oppressive heat and overcrowding in New York City tenements. The children would all stretch out on the dining room floor to sleep. It was a poor man's version of summer camp, but no less fun for the children.

Until the late 1960s, long after Rosie had a home and family of her own, the house she grew up in had no running water. The family used an outhouse that would occasionally need to be moved – a new pit dug, the old one covered up. Wood was the fuel for heating and cooking; it was gathered from nearby woods, chopped and stacked by hand.

They had chickens and pigs and a dairy cow that was milked each morning for cheese, milk and butter. With a family of ten, sometimes 14, I doubt there was ever much left over that had to be kept cold, although they did have an ice box. The ice man who delivered blocks of ice from his truck came every second or third day. Children today purchase ice cream from trucks. In the '30s and '40s, children would run along following the ice man. When he stopped, he would break off ice chips from the blocks that the children sucked on for a refreshing cold treat on hot summer days. It didn't matter that it didn't have cream or sugar or flavoring.

The butcher would come in a horse drawn wagon, similar to today's ice-cream man, showing up on a certain street at a certain time ringing his bell and people would come out to get meat. Rosie shakes her head and mutters -- "out there...in that heat... the flies" – and gives a chuckle and quick shake of her head. Most of their diet was home grown. Eggs gathered, chickens raised then butchered, plucked and cooked. The pigs were generally killed late in the year, after the first frost, after fattening up on corn husks, garden scraps, acorns and pumpkins; the meat salted, dried, cured, and put in the root cellar underground to keep it cold. Fundamentals like flour, sugar and salt were delivered on a regular basis. Instead of each family hopping in their car twice a week to make the trip, the merchant would make one trip through the neighborhood, stopping at each house to deliver enough flour to bake fresh bread for a month.

Rather than building more bedrooms for their growing family, when they could afford to expand, they bought the materials to build a "summer kitchen" apart from the house above the underground root cellar. You didn't need permits, and there was no electricity or plumbing. This second kitchen was a place to cook in the warmer months, to keep the house cool. This was especially important in August- at both the height of the summer heat and the summer harvest. Long days would be spent cooking and canning the excess fruits and vegetables, along with fresh bread that had to be baked every 2-3 days year-round over a wood burning stove. Cooking inside the main house in summer would have made it unbearably hot. They canned tomatoes, cherries, corn, pickled vegetables— whatever was extra. Cauliflower, cabbage, potatoes, apples, and carrots could be stored raw in the cool underground cellar almost indefinitely.

They had fruit trees: peaches, pears, cherries, apples, plums, and even a fig tree that was too delicate to survive New York winters and had to be dug up each year and laid down covered in a thick mound of leaves and old fabric to keep it insulated from frost. Snacks for the kids were kept fresh (or "packaged") by Mother Nature – fresh spring peas in their pods, sunflower and pumpkin seeds in their shells, cherry tomatoes off the vine, fruits off the trees, carrots out of the ground. Nothing went to waste.

When one fruit or another came into season, the neighbors would come over. Two or three families would work together to harvest the fruit as it ripened, turning a full day's work for one or two people into an hour or two shared by 10 people. The men got up on ladders and tossed the fruits down to waiting children with burlap bags. Some would be stored in the root cellar underground to prolong shelf life. Pies would be baked. Excess fruit would be canned in the "summer kitchens" and stored for the winter. Fruits fallen to the ground were scavenged by the chickens, pigs and cow. The family planted cold weather vegetables (like cabbage and kale) in early March, warm weather vegetables (like tomatoes and corn) in May. Their family was famous for their delicious corn, to which they devoted the lion's share of the garden. They would sell the excess for 25 cents a dozen and neighbors would fight to get in early orders to ensure they didn't miss out. They had an arbor of grapes and would make wine each fall, although the wine (at least drinking it) was the domain of the man of the house. They used no pesticides or fertilizers, simply piling waste from the animals, fallen leaves, and organic scraps into a compost heap that would, after sufficient time for it to degrade, be tilled back into the soil at each planting. While they did supplement their own production with items from the market, their regular purchases were flour, sugar, coffee, and tea.

To feed their livestock over winters, they had an arrangement with a wealthy man who owned property about a mile from their home. Rosie's father, Dziadzia (pronounced "jahjah," a diminutive the family patriarch later acquired, short for *dziadzek*, the Polish word for grandfather), would cut this man's fields in the summer with a scythe, doing the man a favor by keeping it neat.

Once the cut vegetation dried for a couple days he would return with the children carrying big burlap sacks that they would fill with the cut dried hay and carry it home on foot. They passed the hay up to Dziadzia in the hay loft, an attic-like space in the top of the barn, where it would be stored to feed the cow in winter and provide insulation in the chicken coop. When that insulation was fouled with excrement, it was removed and replaced with fresh clean straw, and the dirty straw was added to the compost heap to help return nitrogen to the soil in the spring.

Most of the neighbors lived this semi-agrarian/ semi-urban life, and most had large families. They would congregate at the local pond, barely more than "a muddy swamp, but we loved it, it was so nice and cool" to escape the summer heat.

Their mothers not only cooked for 10-14 people each day, but grew the food. Mothers tended the gardens and livestock, then killed, plucked and butchered the meat, baked the bread and took care of the house. This was not a one-woman job. Everyone pitched in with child care, the crops, and helping around the house, but because they were still children it was often made as much a game as could be. Children did not congregate in their own age groups. They were expected to care for and look out for each other and include the younger ones in their play, and, according to Rosie, held no resentments.

Once our interview had covered issues of basic survival, I wondered how yesterday's world compared to the media-saturated, name-brand, Baby Gap, what-type-of-car-drops-you-off-at-school-focused world of today's children and parents. It is not uncommon for children to be competitive or focused on '"fairness" of distribution of goods, or for community members to be concerned with status, to "keep up with the Joneses." I know how this played out in ancient tribal times, and how it plays out today. I wondered how this played out in a small town in upstate NY in the 30s and 40s. Rosie says they did have a car, or rather, "Dziadzia had a car; he was a very proud man." It was the only one in their neighborhood. I'm not sure where he took it, but I heard enough stories of him walking with his children to gather hay or walking six miles with the family to the market to "stock up the pantry," each carrying a bundle back, to understand that the car was not a tool of convenience, but rather a luxury for her father. It's likely the car was used only for social events or occasions, like a nice suit. It was reserved for Sunday drives (yes, this was a pastime) and to go to church. It was a treasured luxury item, and as such, special pains were taken to maintain it and be sure it wasn't "wasted" or "worn out" with daily use.

It seemed as if all of their items were second hand. The house was decorated with only functional and available furniture, the decor coming from textiles that would carefully be sewn into bedspreads or curtains or carefully embroidered pillow covers. Rosie's mother, Babush (the diminutive for grandmother in Polish), loved to make the old look new or the plain look fancy with fine sewing skills and new textiles. Every family had a sewing machine. It was as necessary as a stove or a hammer and saw. More necessary than running water.

All of the children had one or two sets of school clothes, one nice "church" outfit (for two-hour Sunday mass and one-hour Wednesday and Friday night services). In addition to these formal clothes were a jumble of hand-me-downs for all other times, given from family to family and from child to child within the family, but without real ownership. If it fit and it was clean, that's what you wore. When they outgrew their clothes, they would pass them down to the next youngest or to the neighbors. These were primarily boys' clothes, functional and tough. If clothes were torn slightly but still serviceable they were mended or patched. If clothes wore out or were torn badly, they were generally discarded, but not necessarily into the rubbish. They went in the rag pile and were used for cleaning or to shove in gaps to stop drafts, or they were used to insulate the fig tree for the winter.

The girls were all taught to sew at home and in formal classes at school, where they also learned to service and repair the machines. New textiles were more expensive than second hand clothes, so they would not sew new garments from scratch but rather hem or adjust their clothes for fit. They received one new pair of shoes per year, from a charity program for the poor, but those were poor quality and wore out very quickly. Their parents made sure the children picked out the most sensible . . . though the girls would look longingly at the more stylish designs. Good shoes were expensive. They were a poor family with 20 feet among them, so quality shoes, especially for children who would outgrow them, were out of the question. Even at the second-hand store, it was rare to find quality shoes with life left in them because no one threw out good shoes. It didn't matter much to the kids, though, because everyone was poor – all of their friends were in the same boat. And shoes were only worn in winter, anyway. On warm days, kids generally went barefoot.

Rosie and her brothers and sisters were aware of the rich(er) kids, but only peripherally, and they didn't seem to envy them. Nor did they want to move into the rich kids' world of private schools, nice clothes, debutante balls, summer trips to the same resorts, a different church, and fathers who did business together.

I asked Rosie: "What was the one thing you pined for as a child? Was there one thing you can remember a neighbor having that everyone coveted or admired? What was the X-box of 1930s America? A china doll, or a fine set of toy soldiers?"

This took a lot of thought and conversation, and in short the answer was no, nothing. "Toys? What toys?" Rosie and the other kids didn't play with toys – they just played: hopscotch, duck-on-a-rock (one of a myriad versions of tag, each with elaborate rules), kick the can. They climbed trees. Children's imaginations were the fertile well-tended soil from which games sprouted and the source of their later successes in adult life. Kids would imagine, conceptualize, invent, and then they would manipulate and repurpose whatever little material they could access. These skills served them well throughout their lives, at home and in the workforce. They did not have, nor did they want, dolls or trucks. They had real live playmates "coming outta our ears."

Real live playmates were not only other children, but neighborhood strays, injured squirrels found in the woods and nursed back to health, baby chicks. More than once Rosie put a piece of twine on the cow's halter and took her for a walk "like a dog."

Materials for play were everywhere. Kids would stand on hilltops and throw rocks as far as they could, each calling out "I'm Babe Ruth," "No! Mine went farther! I'm Babe Ruth!" They would make kites out of newspaper, glued together and stiffened with paste made from flour and water. With a rueful laugh, Rosie told me, "we'd tie together every scrap of stinkin' string ... we'd save up string for a whole stinking year!" (Before plastic or even paper bags, purchases were delivered tied in a bundle.) Without fail, every time they pooled their carefully scavenged string and finally had enough to fly a kite, one of the knots would come loose or a string would snap and the whole thing would fly away... kite, string, and all. The kite was no loss. It was the string that was irreplaceable.

Rosie was finally able to remember two games that needed toys that couldn't be made from scraps or imagination: sledding and skating. "We had a cheese cutter," a small old fashioned sled on rails, and when it would snow "that thing would go like the wind." It was metal and when it was cold your hands would freeze to it, and it had sharp edges, so if you weren't careful you could get cut, but it was still a treasured object. She is sure they received this second hand also, its exact provenance lost to time. Eight children shared this sled, and you could only ride one at a time "flat on your belly," so they took turns. My favorite part of this story was finding out that they did not get snow days from school. The idea was preposterous. She remembers "snow up past our hips," the

19

neighborhood kids trudging along single file in the wake of one of the bigger kids who would break trail, switching off as they got tired, the younger children in line behind them.

The other cherished childhood toy was ice-skates. "We would go ice-skating on Dinkies pond," and when I asked if they each had their own pair, she answered "more or less. They screwed on to your shoes, so we could all wear them." It didn't seem to matter that they couldn't all wear them at the same time. It was sufficient that they could all have a turn, and as long as you had shoes, the skates would always fit any size foot. They were treacherous, however – and twisted ankles and pinched fingers abounded. Skate keys, small enough for children to lose, were an absolutely necessary tool needed to loosen or tighten the skates to size. A skate key was often as valuable as skates, because a child with a key but no skates could negotiate a turn with the skates from a child with skates but no key. Pooling resources and sharing the benefits of pooled resources was a primary characteristic of their childhood.

I could tell Rosie was having difficulty relating my questions (maybe just my 2015 frame of reference) about consumption and status to her childhood. But all of a sudden, a light bulb went off. Young people and their families did strive for status, she explained, but it was not commercial or materially based. If you had one finely tailored suit, it was impressive, but if you had more you were seen as profligate and indulgent. Status came from school and reference groups. Children vied for the approval of their teachers (who were nuns) and to receive highest marks. They respected and admired each other for doing well and there was fierce competition for the nuns' approval and bragging rights that came with top marks. Adults in the community also received status through their children's good behavior, smarts, work ethic, and virtue, not the size of their wallets. Parents of polite, helpful and hardworking children were admired as "good families."

Rosie still tends an impressive 7-acre property with stunningly beautiful and shockingly productive gardens and a small coop of chickens. You have never lived, you have never eaten, until you've tried a beefsteak tomato the size of a small melon out of her garden or a fresh egg with a yolk that is more to the red side of orange than the yellow. Although she can now get produce from all over the world, she asks "why would I?" She thinks winter tomatoes "stink" and "don't taste like anything." I wondered if she didn't long for more variety. And she again looked at me like I was nuts. Variety? Kale and escarole, sugar snap peas, and carrots in spring, then zucchini and cucumbers and peppers and berries and beans of all kinds, and onions and radishes and zucchini, then tomatoes and corn, then squash and watermelon and pumpkin and apples, then sugar snaps and crisp lettuce again ... all of it grown in rich well-tended soil and picked at the peak of ripeness. Who could want more variety than this? And what good is variety when none of it is ripened on the vine or engineered for taste? She doesn't want her produce to look good, she wants it to taste good.

⌘

Bay Ridge in the 1930s

Samantha Coppola

BROOKLYN, NY

The last 40 years or so in American history is sometimes collectively and proudly referred to by its contemporaries as the "information age." This title has many positive connotations attached to it. In fact, it would be very difficult to argue that more information does not equate to more progress. Yet, if we are currently living in a new age defined by an abundance of information, knowledge, and technology, then how did we define the age before this one? Was there a dark age to our enlightenment period? What was life like 50 years ago and are we so much better off today? Meaning, what was the standard of living a generation or two ago and how does it compare to our current quality of life?

In this paper I explore what it means to at least one person to have grown up in this mysterious age before the world was permanently changed by the digital revolution and all of its consequences. My interviewee is a woman named Yvonne, 83 years old and probably the healthiest and most active person over 60 I have ever known. She is very kind and intelligent, well-read (she reads the news every day and I am not talking about the Post or the Daily News), and she always has something valuable to say. Yvonne is one of my mother's closest friends and is so important to us that I call her my unofficial Godmother.

One morning over coffee and her usual dry toast with the imported French ("100% all-natural ingredients") Bonne Maman jelly she brings from home, Yvonne and I sat in a small diner in our hometown of Bay Ridge, Brooklyn, New York. At certain times throughout the day there is a real sense of community in this diner. The older generation have lived here for at least half of a century, and Yvonne is part of this community.

I begin my interview wondering many things. I did not write down any formal questions for fear of limiting the conversation. My hope is that Yvonne naturally opens up about what is important and remarkable to her and that she steer the conversation in any direction she so chooses. With less than a few prompts from me Yvonne does not disappoint.

The very first thing I observe is the pride she feels for her generation. She does not simply list the difference between then and now, she brags about them. Early on in the interview she confirms this air of pride that I have already picked up by plainly stating, "I'm glad I grew up during those times; there was a different mindset."

I believe that understanding that different mindset is crucial but can be difficult. Several times throughout the interview Yvonne stops and asks me with questioning eyes, "Can you imagine? I mean can you picture what I'm saying to you?" She doesn't think I can, and while I would like to think that completing a history major, reading *A Tree Grows in Brooklyn* (twice), and watching countless very old movies set in old New York is enough background so that I can understand what life was like for Yvonne... it's not. Sure, I can picture it, but can I truly imagine what it was like to live in a community with a totally different mindset? What was that mindset and how is it different from that of my own generation?

According to Yvonne the people of her childhood in 1930s Brooklyn were more neighborly and had a lot more respect for each other. She still cannot get used to how individualistic our society has become since then. In fact, Yvonne had just experienced something a few days prior to our interview that proved her point. When shopping in a small store Yvonne had observed a child knock something off of a shelf. When Yvonne asked the child to put the item back on the shelf the mother became irate with her. According to the child's mother, Yvonne (who, by the way, is in no way a rude or crass woman), had no right to speak to her child that way. Yvonne had no choice but to back down as the woman huffed and puffed about old women minding their own business. Totally. Different. Mindset. As early as a generation or two ago it was the norm for people to look out for and even discipline each other's kids. Mothers and fathers of all ages were highly respected by children and their parents alike.

On the topic of children, Yvonne also has strong feelings about today's school system. She remembers only having class 6 months out of the year and a short school day. Each day all of the children at her school went home for lunch! To think that nobody ate at school is incredible to me. The school lunch program in New York City today is invaluable. Not only do many students depend on the free or reduced price school meals, but the schools also depend on the children who receive those meals in order to get funding!

Another difference Yvonne shared with me was the nature of the classes in schools back then. She liked the idea that schools "rounded you" as a child with classes like cooking and wood work. Now she feels that schools do not do a good job teaching children useful life skills or even how to think for themselves.

Aside from school Yvonne has many fond memories of her leisure time as a kid. She recalls walking to the park by herself because the neighborhood felt safer then. With matter-of-fact confidence she states that "there were no fears" back then. This is in stark contrast to our society today, which enforces laws like "Stand Your Ground." As a child Yvonne ran around outside and played in the street every day because there were very few cars.

She remembers having fresh milk delivered to her home and a horse and buggy that would come to her block carrying farm fresh fruits and vegetables for sale. Fruit was her dessert and it was a real treat when the ice cream man came to her block on summer days. Yvonne believes these were the reasons why "everyone was thin" so many years ago. She says the children made their own fun and the only thing she remembers ever buying was comic books. In comparison to today this is indeed hard to imagine.

"Kids didn't ask for things because it wasn't there." Unlike today, "there were not a lot of products and no TV or advertisements to put pressure on consumers like there is now."

There has also been a significant change in our culture. Yvonne thinks it is very simple, "spending wasn't the thing to do." She emphasizes the importance of living according to your means and that you should spend if you can afford it. However, most people back then could not afford it, so they simply did not spend. Currently that is not the case for this generation. Many factors contributed to this change including the availability of credit cards and the pressure put on people to make them believe they need the newest version of every piece of technology available.

There are many lovely things about the era Yvonne grew up in and it is no wonder she is so proud of her past. There are also many extraordinary and positive things that define the "information age" we are now in. Yet, as we observe the rapid development of our communities, dramatic changes in society, and the consistent growth of a capitalist world economy, we have to ask ourselves: is this sustainable? Can we maintain the standard of living we are now used to? It is a tough question, and Yvonne might just be around long enough to witness the potentially devastating consequences of an unsustainable culture. In fact, I believe we are all already aware of the risks associated with mass consumption and rapid development. There is a lot we need to consider. An analysis of the recent past could be one place to start, thus making Yvonne's story and others like hers very useful to my generation.

⌘

What'd You Kids Do for Fun, Pop?

Samantha Bright

STATEN ISLAND, NY

I had a really nice time talking with my father. Hearing stories of his childhood made me realize how different his childhood was and how much he tried to give us. When I was a child, our family went somewhere every summer, usually camping. We had birthday parties and great Christmases. In other words, my siblings and I cannot complain, and believe me, we don't.

My father recalled having bunk beds that they bought from Port Richmond Avenue, so all the boys had their own bed. The pillows were a different story; there were four boys but only three pillows. The youngest boy would always get a pillow and the older three would have to take turns sharing. Eventually my dad found a bargain store that sold pillows for a dollar and begged my grandmother to get them.

Then there was the couch they bought for $10 at a garage sale. This story in particular had us laughing hysterically. The couch was crooked and was held up by books, so when the kids had to take their books to school the couch was crooked until they came back. Their one television had broken knobs, so they changed the channel with a pair of pliers. The picture would roll, and to make it stop they would throw shoes at the TV. They straightened out a wire clothes hanger to replace the broken antenna.

I asked Pop what he and his siblings did for fun. They played tag, Johnny Buck Buck, Red Rover Red Rover, and other games that did not require anything other than themselves. Sometimes my grandmother would send the boys outside with spoons and they would just spend the day digging in the yard. "Then we'd come inside, wash the spoons, and use them for dinner. They were all bent."

My father noted how his childhood was so different from mine in terms of life in general. He talked about how they used to leave after breakfast and be gone all day, his parents never knowing where they were, and then just come home for dinner. That never happened when I was growing up; we didn't leave the block without letting one of my parents know.

It shocks me sometimes to hear these stories about his childhood, simply because my grandmother today doesn't remotely resemble the woman from his stories. This is where the majority of our laughs came from: "Can you imagine grandma sending you and your brother to do laundry down on Port Richmond Avenue at five years old?" No, I cannot.

⌘

Children Now Are at a Disadvantage

Ashley DiCrescento

I interviewed my Grandmother Elaine at her house in Sayreville, New Jersey. My Grandma grew up in Park Slope, Brooklyn, in a three-bedroom house along with five siblings. Growing up, my Grandma and her siblings had many chores to take care of around the house while my great grandpa and great grandma were off at work.

Grandma loved when she got the chance on the weekends to go to her father's garden.

> My father used to take coffee grounds and teach me to put them in the soil to help fertilize the dirt; he also put coffee grounds in his potato skins as well. We grew our own tomatoes and gathered them all together to mash up and mix herbs and spices into our homemade sauce.

On hot summer days all the kids from my Grandma's block would get together and cool off by using the water from fire hydrants on the block. They would spend hours playing stickball in the street and a hide and seek game called "coco leavio." They swam in community pools, rode bamboo bicycles, and played with dolls.

> One of my brothers took a wooden crate and made it into a scooter to ride down the streets. He took an old fashioned adjustable skate and unscrewed the middle part, detaching the wheels from it and used another piece of wood on the top as handle bars.

Grandma's chores included getting the towels from the wash machine and putting them through rollers to get rid of the excess water. Afterwards, she had to hang the clothes outside to dry on a clothesline that was attached from the house to the telephone pole. She liked being in the kitchen with her mother.

> Not only did my mother make her own chopped meat but she also baked a lot and taught me how to make cheesecake, bread pudding, rice pudding, and tapioca.

It was interesting to know how much of a passion my great grandma had for baking and how she was always coming up with new recipes to make for special occasions with her family. As she got older she passed those recipes down to her daughter, my grandma.

The stories my grandma told me about how her brothers came up with new ways to build their own toys and scooters was pretty cool. Today children rely so much on technology they would probably not even know where to start when it came down to having to build their own scooters. Children now are at a disadvantage trying to have a real childhood, one that's based on real toys and not on smart phones. Back then children had to make fun out of what they had.

⌘

My Grandfather Is Green

Deja Richardson

NEW YORK METROPOLITAN REGION

As Americans we take advantage of the easy accessibility and abundance of the things we consume. We don't have to distinguish needs from wants. Life 50 years ago was drastically different. The differences between the generations are flabbergasting and things are only going to get worse.

In this research paper I conducted an interview with my grandfather, Albert, 77, who gave me information on what life was like 50 years ago. I also talked to the new generation on how they see the changes from 50 years ago to today. Many don't agree with the way of living now but believe they have no choice.

My grandfather, a Vietnam War veteran, explained that back then things were pricy because the quality was authentic and very fine. "Money was valued more. It seems like the value of the dollar decreases every day now," he said, adding that a twenty dollar bill back then felt like having a fifty dollar bill today. "I spent my money wisely," he told me, and "always kept my belongings in tip top shape."

In order to distinguish the needs from the wants, it was essential to determine how you were going to survive a brutal cold winter or scorching hot summer. Cooling and heating systems were quite different back then my grandfather told me his parents used to harvest snow during winter and store it so they could use it for the summer to stay cool. Not only did people use ice to stay cool, but they also stored food (milk, butter, etc.) in ice to preserve it. During the winter many homes had fire places. The men would chop wood for the winter all fall long so they would not run out.

People back then knew the importance of preserving and saving. Look inside a garbage can today; you'll see papers, bottles, boxes, clothes, old accessories, and just about anything you can think of. Fifty years ago, items of high value would not be thrown away so easily. "Everything was fixable." The way of life was literally reuse, reduce, recycle. If there was a hole in my grandfather's pants his mother would patch it up for him. He would re-wear that shirt and eventually pass it down. What are "hand-me-downs," if not an example of valuing the concept of reduce, reuse, recycle?

It was a part of the community to do for others and help others when they needed help.

> We gave old baby clothes to mothers expecting, gave away the kids clothes when they grew into adults and couldn't fit them anymore. I still feel as though that aspect of my life stuck with me. Nothing changed.

I'm fully involved in the raising of my grandchildren, I see them every day and love them like my own, just like my mother did for her grandchildren. The only difference is that the kids are in daycare from basically infancy to adolescence, so I see them after 3pm. But I believe that the upbringing and community that I grew up in influenced my way of life now.

The change from agriculture to industrial work styles gave people a chance to express themselves and caused an opening for leisure time, but working class families, especially black families, knew that leisure time just didn't come so easily to them. The only ones that really enjoyed leisure and didn't have to stress were children. Because they didn't have an important work role to play in the family, children had time to roam about and explore.

Children used to stay outside until the street lights came on. Growing up as a child I myself was outside all day running around, interacting with friends, playing in dirt, getting dirty, etc. I was a child and that was expected of me and that was literally ten years ago. When the streetlights came on I knew it was time to come in the house and by that time I was glad of it because running all day made me tired. Nowadays children stay inside and engage in playing video games. They would rather watch children play online than actually play with real children.

Outdoor activities like hop scotch, ball games, tag, skipping, ring-a-ring o' roses, and others were very popular back then. One of my grandfather's favorite games was piggy in the middle, a ball game. Most of the time children played at school during play time. They used their wits to create their own toys, or they shared toys or played with hand-me-down toys. A popular handheld game back then was the whip and tip. Playing in-house with marbles also kept children occupied.

My grandfather said the way of life back then was much "slower." It was harder in that resources weren't as widely available as they are now, especially for him as a young black man, but he realizes now that when he needed to slow down he could.

Though he's from the older generation, my grandfather has a sense of the problems of today, like global warming. "I can't determine whether it's spring or winter," my grandfather joked. "It's all messed up." He doesn't like how we're killing the earth. He thought we should do away with phones just a little – they're a really big distraction – and people should go outside and plant a tree instead.

> Trees bring oxygen. It can help with the effects of global warming. It won't reverse it, but it'll sure help.

The old way of living was definitely a better way of life. We have to become a sustainable society again. We have to realize that there are generations behind us and we have to get the generation before us to help with the movement. We have to save the Earth and become aware of how what we do we affects society.

⌘

Everyone Should Pick Up the Gardening Habit

Yasman Yudeh

BROOKLYN, NY, AND PALESTINE

When I entered Kamila's [not her real name] home, the air was filled with a scent of fresh mint tea and spinach pies baking in the oven. Kamila enjoys company and is showing her appreciation with food. She started our conversation by telling me about having an arranged marriage in Palestine and leaving her family to move to Brooklyn, NY in the 1960s. Coming from a poor village in Palestine, she was used to depending on family members and neighbors for survival. But in America she knew only her husband, though more relatives arrived over the years.

Perhaps it was because they came from poor families that Kamila and her husband tried not to waste anything. Most of the furniture in their home throughout the 60s, 70s and 80s was picked up from the street or given to them by relatives. Kamila remembers when recycling first started in the late

1980s, but she herself had been recycling long before that, using large cans for plants. Kamila still seals holes in household items with tape and continues to use items long after a more "wasteful" person would have thrown them out. These habits probably help explain why the couple were able to save money and give their children a better life.

For as long as they've been married, Kamila's husband has grown fruits and vegetables in their backyard, and they still enjoy raising plants as a leisure activity. She thinks gardening is a habit everyone should pick up, because it's good for the environment and for our health. Kamila, aware that plants use carbon dioxide and release oxygen into the atmosphere, is proud that she once hired someone to cut through the concrete sidewalk to plant a tree in front of the house.

⌘

Chasing the Ice Man

Myrtle Wangerin (as told to the editors)

MILWAUKEE, WISCONSIN

Myrtle Wangerin was born in Milwaukee, Wisconsin, about 1919. Despite being in a somewhat prosperous middle-class family, she grew up in what we today would call a sustainable lifestyle that was not much different from other families in the city. She had only 2-3 outfits: a Sunday dress, summer and winter clothes, and every year some new school clothes. When she would outgrow the clothes, the next child or cousin would use it.

Myrtle's family always repaired the clothes if they were torn rather than buying new ones, and the same with socks. It was her mother's job to darn and repair the torn heels or toes of the socks, using a small gourd inside the sock to create a surface over which to darn. Her mother, Ruth's grandma, was still darning socks that way in the 1960s.

THIS DRESS IS STILL IN THE FAMILY

Myrtle remembers having 2-3 pairs of shoes, to which they'd add a strip of metal on the toe and heel of the sole to make them last forever. "These were all leather shoes," she said. Those shoes would last a long time because every time they had a hole or tear, the shoe man would repair them.

At Christmas her mother would buy a doll, her grandmother would make the dress for it, and she would dress up the doll. Dollhouse furniture would pass on from grandparents and parents to their kids.

"People mostly consumed local fruits and vegetables," she said. There were truck farmers who would go around the town and sell fresh produce from their farms around the city. (Davoud's sister, who was about the same age as Myrtle, also said that all greens and vegetables used to come from near her city, Tehran.) In addition, there was a market for the truck farmers in town; there were no supermarkets—only small local and individually owned stores.

"You bought only what you needed," Myrtle stressed. They would also can (preserve) vegetables for the winter.

Many people had cast-iron stoves for cooking and heating the house, though they used coal, since her father ran a coal delivery business.

They owned an icebox to cool the food, which had a compartment for a block of ice. The iceman would come around with ice blocks in a truck. She and her friends would follow the truck and ask him to give them a piece of ice to chew on.

She said at that time there were both streetcars and trolleys, but later on buses (both public and privately owned) replaced them.

⌘

I'm Jealous in a Weird Way of the Life My Mother Lived

Teresa Alejandro

SOUTH BRONX, NY

Although we have seemed to evolve in every arena, from music to fashion to politics, what has perhaps changed the most is our collective attitude towards consumption.

My mother, who was born in Puerto Rico but brought to New York as a child, was raised in a very low-income neighborhood in the South Bronx. Now sixty years old and a lower middle class working woman, a housing manager in fact, she can look back and distinguish how very different her youth was to the life she and my family share now.

She remembered one of the highlights from her childhood: at nine years old her family got a television for the first time, a small black and white portable TV. She remembers how exciting this was because it was one of the first televisions to pick up the Spanish stations. It was a big hit in her building and neighbors from every floor would come down into her family's apartment to watch it, as they didn't have sets of their own. She remembers every evening her mother making hot chocolate and cheese and crackers for their guests as they sat down to watch telenovelas together. It is hard to imagine all my neighbors and friends having to come over to share a television with my family today, but the idea seems kind of exciting to be honest, because that just means that we would be together much more than we are currently, not to mention how much cost it would save to pool our resources.

At the same time, having one week's worth of outfits seems to have been unheard of. However, I can appreciate the simplicity of those days when they did not have to spend hours deciding what to wear every time they wanted to walk out of the house. As far as my mother remembers, she only lived around other people in her economic class, poor people, and as she says everyone lived that way so no one knew any different. Their consumption was purely based on need, with little time or money to entertain wants. They just had the "basic clothes."

As for cooling themselves in the summer, aside from a fan, she and her sisters often slept outside on the fire escape to stay even cooler. As for the winter, my grandfather was a super and therefore my mother's family always lived in the basement next to the boiler. Because of where they lived, the winters were always warm. My mother remembers the coal for the furnace being delivered every day and she and her sisters would play in the heap until they turned black. Food was kept in a basic refrigerator at the time. Overall, the basement kept them cool in the summer and warm in the winter. When I think about the way my mother's family heated and cooled their home.

When I asked my mother how she got around, her answer was simple: walking, everywhere. Her school was diagonally across the street, their shopping area was two blocks in one direction, and church was four blocks in the other. She only recalls taking the subway once a year to visit in. Her family never owned a car; she didn't in fact until she married my father. What a contrast to the two, and at one point three, cars my family owns now. I cannot imagine having to walk every day to school or shopping or much of anywhere really, and I honestly cannot picture my mother doing so today either. It is amazing to think that once upon a time she had to do that considering how dependent she is on her car today.

My mom remembers there being less waste when she was young than we produce today. Because plastic and Styrofoam were not really used, so garbage was mostly food products. And a lot of the food scraps were fed to the dog that lived in the basement with her family.

When she was a kid, my mom said she and her sisters used chalk to play hopscotch and jumped rope with the clothing line. She distinctly remembers her and her mother playing jacks together. One of her prized possessions when she was young was a Chatty Cathy doll she received one year for Christmas. They usually didn't get gifts like this, so she was really excited to receive it.

Hide and seek was also a really popular game for them. All games were played out on the street. Though she didn't really have many toys aside from perhaps the doll, they were gendered and she only received things targeted towards girls. All other play things she had weren't gender colored or specific.

When it comes to toys, I can draw a SHARP line. As a little kid, I had one of the biggest Barbie collections I've ever seen. Not having those to play with my sisters at the time would have changed my whole childhood; I cannot picture what it would have come to.

In New York City my mom just remembers there being a lot of concrete. Living in the South Bronx, she recalls, she didn't see many trees, and this as well has not changed too much. The only open green space my mother remembers was St. Mary's park which they had to walk to, though this park still exists today, it has gotten smaller: She remembers clearly being able to see the stars at night. Today, the stars have become almost impossible to make out at night.

When my mother was young, her community was very closely knit. She remembers everyone looking after everyone. Her godmother knew everyone on the block. This came in particularly helpful one time when my mother's family was robbed. Her godmother knew who had done it. She gathered up all the men from the neighborhood with her to go after him and successfully got everything back. Again, her godmother was once looking out the window checking up on everyone and was able with other neighbors to save one of the boys from the building who was having an epileptic attack; she just yelled out and everyone came to the rescue. It was more like a family, my mother said. Everyone knew everyone and looked out for each other. Today this has changed since she's moved to the suburbs. She's too busy working to really know her neighbors well.

Overall, I believe that though modern times have brought great innovation, the old way of life that my mother was a part of reaped much greater rewards. The community aspect alone that stemmed from the economic status of the neighborhood is in my opinion the most important. The feeling of responsibility to care for the environment and community you are a part of is significantly intensified if you are actively part of that community and are invested in the wellbeing of those you share it with.

Also as previously mentioned, though I won't dare complain about the luxuries that my parents have been able to give me, I feel that living the way my mother did, without excess, would make living in today's world so much less stressful and competitive. Though it's not really feasible anymore, walking rather than driving would be easier because it is so much more cost effective and healthier for you and your environment. Today our cars and air conditioners and cell phones make our lives more convenient but in the bigger picture they simply aren't necessities.

I admire the life that my mother lived and in some weird ways I'm jealous of it. She seemed to have been so happy with relatively so little. That's easier said than done in our society now. The way of life she described was so much friendlier to the environment without her even knowing it at the time. Some of the common-sense practices from the time not only made sense for their lives but were just the thing to keep the environment clean and happy as well; a lesson we'd be smart to learn today.

⌘

PART TWO: LATIN AMERICA AND THE CARIBBEAN

Treat People the Way You Want to Be Treated

Jeff Fernandez

Dominican Republic

Story telling is big in my family, especially for the older folks. When we all get together we're probably going to hear another crazy story from the old days in the Dominican Republic. I often think how crazy and mind blowing those days must have been. In the age of technology where most of us have cell phones, computers, tablets and other electronic devices, the older people in my family remember a time when the only modern technology they had was maybe a radio.

There was always food on *my* table, but not always on my *dad's* when he was young. I decide to ask him the story of his life. My father gets home from work tired and hungry around 11 o'clock pm. He takes off his St. Louis Cardinals hat, puts it on the dining room table, grabs some fruit that my mother has cut up for him, goes to the couch, kicks off his boots, and flicks on channel 41 where they show the Hispanic news. It's been the same routine every day for the past thirty years, I'm pretty sure.

My dad's story starts in the small municipality of Sanchez in the province of Samaria in the Dominican Republic. Bernardo Antonio was born in 1958, the 5th of nine children. My grandmother was a midwife and made clothes for a living, and my grandfather worked the fields chopping sugar cane and planting other fruits and veggies like most men in the Dominican Republic back then.

Their house was made out of logs, branches, hardened mud, rocks, and sheets of steel for a roof. There were three rooms in the whole house: my grandparents' bedroom, a make-shift kitchen, and the one room for all nine kids. My dad and his brothers and sisters didn't have any beds; they all slept on the floor on blankets my grandmother made for them. There was no bathroom; if you needed to use the bathroom you had to go outside.

They would take baths with the water they collected from the rain. Little children in the countryside in the Dominican Republic almost never wore clothes. My dad told me he didn't get a pair of pants till he was about 4 years old. He would just walk around naked from age one to three. You still see this today in the really poor neighborhoods in the Dominican Republic.

My dad never lets me hear the end of how hard he's worked in his life. When I ever complained about having a long day at work or school he would tell me,

> Why are you tired – that's not work! You haven't worked like I worked! I started working when I was seven for Christ sake! In the fields! In the sun! With a smelly donkey who never listened to me!

While your grandfather whipped me! So don't complain to me about work!

My dad told me about the days that he would have to walk miles with his donkey to go deliver some clothing that my grandmother had made for somebody. It was like taking a donkey from Staten Island to Long Island. He would make trips like that all the time, but he was never afraid because people were really nice back then. On these trips random people he didn't even know would ask my dad if he needed food to eat or shelter for the night.

There was no such thing as throwing something out in my dad's family. Everyone wore hand me downs, even hand me down underwear. Any banana peels, apple cores, or bones they would throw out were given to the pigs to eat, so there was never any garbage outside. For water they would collect rainwater in huge tubs, or they would go to the river miles away to get water. That reminds me of the day my father gave me one of the biggest beatings of my life; at seven years old, I didn't know you couldn't pee in the river.

As my dad, aunts, and uncles got older they were able to move to the city of Santiago, where my grandparents still live today, in a big fancy house that my dad bought for them. My dad still doesn't own a cell phone; he wouldn't even know what to do with one if he had it. To my dad, life is about working hard and providing for your family. He believes in the importance of saving your money and never throwing out food or clothes. Treat people the way you would want to be treated and respect everyone, he always told me.

We finished the interview, and the night ended like it always does, with my dad passed out on the couch and the news watching him instead of the other way around. He'll get up at six in the morning to do it all over again.

⌘

Mom, What is a Coal Pot?

Latasha Hughes

ANTIGUA, WEST INDIES

Walking back into the house after taking my 5-year-old nephew to school for 8 o'clock, I was dragged right back out by my mother. It was a Friday and it was raining off and on again. One word to describe my morning was "HELL." There were no classes for me. All I wanted to do was sleep. With a sad face on and water in my shoes I followed my mother to a Chinese supermarket name Chug Li. Li sells a whole bunch of things you wouldn't be able to find in a regular supermarket. For instance, Dragon fruit and black chicken.

Don't take this as me being an ungrateful child. I kicked and screamed as a joke. I love this woman and I would do anything for her. We laughed and joked around a lot as we were there.

After we finished and were leaving, we called a cab. We got in and as usual I asked my mum a lot of questions about her life back in Antigua, West Indies, and how it is different than up here.

Why did you guys use a copper pot to catch the water?

It comes from ancient times. Been doing it for a long time. I don't know the full history behind it. It's like a tank and it keeps cool at night time and it's called 'good water.'

We used to use what is called a copper pot to fill up the water. It has a hole that the pipe can go in so that nothing else can blow in it. The rain falls in the pipe and then down into the copper pot. The water that we use is the rain water. It's what we back home call good water. We put a net at the bottom of the pipe so not to have dirt, leaves or anything else fall in the water.

Mum, what is a coal pot? I know that it's made of clay, but does it do anything special? Does it look different than a regular pot?

We use coal pot. It's made from clay. Back home we burn our own [char]coal. We cut down wood and dig a big hole and put the wood in there. Then cover it with hay and dirt and we leave out a hole where we light it and the wood stays under there and turns into [char]coal. When it's finished then we dig it up, bag the coal, and sell it or we use some of it to cook.

My aunt Naldeen had one. It's made from clay and you (as I said) put coal inside of it and then you light it with a match so the fire will be able to catch. You can put oil on the coal and put a piece of paper under the coal and then you gather the coal and light the paper. It's similar to a BBQ coal but we would chop down trees to make our coal.

If we were to go back there, Mum, can you show me how to do it? Do people still do it down there?

> Some people still do it in the countryside but now they have stove and stuff but people still have the coal pot along with the stove. Like some people fry their fish outside on the coal pot instead of....

Oh, does it taste better than cooked on the stove?

> Yeah the food on the coal pot taste much better than if it's cooked on the stove. You can cook rice and regular food on it.

Why did you guys bake your own bread? Isn't the bread at the store easier and less work on your part?

> Yeah, but sometimes people want to make their own. It's a lot fresher and we don't know where the store bread is coming from.

How did you guys make your bread?

> With flour yeast and lard. We make it in a brick oven that we would build ourselves or a regular oven. We made it like you would make dumpling. We would use our hands. We would let the dough sit for a while and then in an hour time we would form out the bread and then we would put it in the brick oven with wood because we didn't have gas back then.

Are there different toys that we have today that you didn't have? I don't know if you notice but there are dolls now that poop and things like that. Did you have anything like that?

> No, we didn't. We had educational toys.

HA HA. What kind of educational toys? HAHAH

"Kisses teeth." I think you have it here. It's a wood toy with beads on it like when you're learning how to count and you're going back and....

THE ABACUS!

We had those.

Knowing what I know about my mum's life after talking to her that day, she raised my sisters and me the way she was raised. There are just a few differences in the way she taught us and how other people raise their children. An example is that in our house in the Bronx we have buckets for the days we need to catch water. The water that we fill in our buckets is used for us to take showers, brush our teeth and anything that requires the use of water.

⌘

My Mom Still Plays Jacks—and She's Good!

Lucia Rossi

PERU

During the interview I did for anthropology class, my mother, Ana Marlene, seemed to get most passionate about the question about *Children and Toys*. This doesn't surprise me because my mother truly is young at heart. Although she is a very forgetful person, she remembered these moments of her childhood as if she was still in Peru.

> I used to play with the soda caps and make furniture. I flattened it, folded it and made tables and chairs. I don't remember how we did it.
>
> We played jump rope and Jacks and we played "The Statue" game. You went on a table or something high, and you had to stand there like a statue and not move. Everyone would have to try to make the statue laugh. It was five girls who used

to play. If you laughed, you lost and would have to do whatever they said.

Children played in the streets. The boys played soccer. Some kids were so poor that they used to make the ball themselves. They would stuff it with clothing and wrap it up around with nylon pantyhose. The poor kids played with that in the middle of the street. They [young Peruvians] were not great in other sports because they didn't have the money for equipment like hockey masks and pads. Soccer, you don't need anything but a ball. The Americans here are so spoiled.

At this point in the interview my mom went upstairs to her bedroom, went through her clothes drawers, and actually got her jacks. She sat on the wooden floor in our living room and actually started playing.

I used to play so much jacks that my knees were black because the cement was so rough, but that's what we did in school a lot. See, I'm still good!

She bounced the ball and grabbed the jacks with ease in front of me.

Usually we got toys for Christmas. My best toy was the dolls. I played with dolls and I even christened my dolls. I picked a godmother and a godfather for my dolls. The godmother made the dress for my doll, a pink dress. A poor kid who made money by picking up garbage for people living in a building was the godfather to my doll. I felt bad for him because he was poor and that day he showed up very clean for the christening party. We had a great time and we even had pastries for the party. We had favors with the godparents' names and parents' names. We called them "Capillos." It was like a fancy name tag. The party was very fancy. I was only seven years old. We played like grownups. I remember that kid.

⌘

Aunque Teniamos Poco, Vivimos Feliz!*

Lesley Bonilla

GUADALAJARA, MEXICO

It was a windy day in Manhattan as I sat cozily on the couch alongside my grandmother and mom dipping Maria cookies in a cup of coffee. We were keeping warm from the biting wind that was fighting its way through the cracks of the window. My grandmother, who is currently visiting New York from Guadalajara, Mexico, loves telling stories of her youth.

My grandmother raised her children in a little town in Mexico called Concepcion de Bramador, which was commonly called "La Concha" by the residents of the town.

> It was a very simple life, air free and just natural. It was a small rural community very isolated from other towns, so most of the community was family.

---

* Although we had little, we lived happy.

65

We were surrounded by huge mountains, enjoying the weather that never got too hot or too cold.

I turned to my mom and asked what she did for fun.

I would go to the fields where my dad worked or I swam in rivers that had beautiful waterfalls. Oh yeah, I also had a doll; she had an eye missing but she was my favorite toy.

My grandmother and mom spoke about how food wasn't necessarily scarce since everything was always available right in their backyard or from neighbors, though it was true that food was rationed. There were never any leftovers because the food available was divided among nine people. A typical meal consisted of vegetables, tortillas, frijoles (beans) and cheese made from milk from the family cow. Red meat was a big deal since they could only afford it once a month, if lucky. The majority of their food was grown on my grandparent's property. They had fruit trees such as orange, guava and mango. They owned a field of *maiz* (corn) and also grew coffee beans.

We owned a couple of cows, which we used for milk, a donkey that was used to carry corn from the fields and wood for fire. We had many chickens, too.

As soon as my grandmother mentioned chickens, my mom interrupted,

We ate every part of the chicken, literally every part, even the feet, which I always got stuck with!

I recognized that everything was hands-on and no one was afraid of getting his or her hands dirty. Even the furniture around the house was handmade. Families made shelves from bamboo and beds that didn't have mattresses but were really flat pieces of wood with blankets on top of it. They even made traditional handicrafts to sell.

There was a fair where people sold gum figurines. My dad and I would take the chicle (sap) from the sapodilla tree, which at first looked like milk. We washed it and pulled at it until it turned to gum that can be made into figures. We made all sorts of figures such as mini fruits and vegetables. Once the figures were made we would paint them and bring them to the next town over and sell them there.

All in all, the life of my grandparents, my mother and her siblings was sustainable and in my opinion a better way of living than today. Although they weren't as privileged growing up as today's generation with certain materialistic things, I believe it was a much healthier lifestyle. They knew exactly where the food they were eating came from, whereas today we often don't know what is inside our store bought food. They were always active, whether it was for work or just for fun. As my grandmother put it, *"Aunque teniamos poco, vivimos feliz"* [Although we had little, we lived happy.]

⌘

Why Spend Money to Buy Fish?

Clover Matthews

JAMAICA

On March 30, 2016 at about 6:30 pm I had an opportunity to interview Landford Ricketts, my eighty-year-old landlord.

When I entered their apartment, Mr. Ricketts had just finished supper. He said, "You want to have some dinner?" I answered, "No thank you, sir." He said, "How about a drink?" I accepted his offer because I knew he would have one, too, and that would give him more courage to talk.

He began,

> My parents have eleven of us, eight boys and three girls. There were thirteen of us in our family. Time was hard. They did not have a big house, so my mother and the girls sleep in the main house and my father and the older boys sleep in a small house in the yard close to the main house that also serve to store surplus foods and supplies.

My father work for himself. He was a farmer. He grow all kind of foods: plantains, bananas, tomatoes, scallions, cassavas, pumpkins, oranges, yams, four different type of potatoes, watermelons. He sells to the fairs, churches, and to people that buy and sell from other neighboring communities. He owned a lot of land – about four acres that we live on and another five acres about four miles away where he raised lot of cows, goats, pigs, and chickens. My father employed a lot of workers to work on the farms. He let us work on the farm on the weekends and before we go to school in the mornings. Sometimes when he got a big order we would not go to school; we would go to the farm and work.

What about food?

My father would kill a pig every weekend for us to eat. We would store it in a barrel with salt and pimento seeds to preserve it. We smoked it over the fire because we did not have a refrigerator. We only ate what we grow because my father refuse to buy any other kind of food that he did not grow. If we want to have fish for dinner, he said, "Why should I spend money to buy fish? When I start a fish farm you will eat all the fish you want."

My mother was a midwife. She delivered all of her children by herself and also helped other women. She knew what kind of herbal medicine women should use from the trees in and around the community before and after the delivery.

By interviewing my landlord and remembering conversations with my own father, I learned that people from different parts of Jamaica lived a similar lifestyle, relying on cultivation, livestock and trade work. Mr. Ricketts mentioned that they reused everything and that they did not have much, just what they needed. That's just exactly what my father told me.

⌘

YOU KNEW BOB MARLEY?!

Courtney Tucker

JAMAICA

Grandmother always said, "You Americans have life too easy. You should've been born down a yard!" So, in what turned out to be a hysterical interview, I set out to see if she was right. I'm writing it down the way she really said it, so you can hear her Jamaican voice.

She answered some questions about practical things first:

> One chore of mine was to get wood to cook food. Back then we never had gas stove. Chop them up, bundle them up, and tie them up, put them on your cotter (a cloth) on your head and go over and under wire to carry them home. You make up your fire in the house and cook. Sometimes we would have to climb up trees and cut the wood off of trees.

Q: How were you able to tell time back then?

We had a plane that used to fly over our district every morning. That's how you knew it was about 4am. Every morning you would hear the roosters and crows and that's how you can tell it was early morning

Q: How many shoes did you own?

One pair to go to school and go to church. Whoever never had shoes would rub down in coconut oil and shine your feet and go to Sunday school same way.

Q: What kind of toys you had growing up?

TOY! Mommy always cut off daddy pants foot and made dolls for us. Or we had gig. The "gig" (a "top") was one of my favorite toys growing up. Usually I made it from scratch with branches from the Lignum Vitae tree. We use a sharp knife to shave it down and shape it at the same time. Then we smooth it off with sandpaper. When the sanding is done, we put a nail in the bottom for the point and you have your gig. Wrap your cord around it and you're ready to play. Similar to a yo-yo. My brothers loved playing with marbles but we loved those homemade toys.

Q: Let's talk about dating?

I never liked the whole dating thing because I was afraid to go out at night. The place was so dark, and back then we did not have any electricity to light outside. How we made lamps was you get your soda bottle, throw some oil in it, put paper and that was your torch lamp.

Q: Describe your favorite music back then.

When I grew up and moved out and moved to Kingston with your mother I would always listen to this music from the man that lived in the house back of mines. Every night you would hear this man and his people make music and smoke weed. From night till morning Bob Marley would be in his yard making music. It was the sweetest sound though sometimes I wanted to curse him.

Q: YOU KNEW BOB MARLEY?!

Did I know the man?! When mango time come he would come to my yard and ask to pick some and no matter how many times I tell him to take, don't need to ask, he would still knock on my door and ask to pick the fruit off my tree. So nice he was, but lord would he keep us up all night with his music.

Listening to my grandmother's stories, I finally understood what she meant about me "living in luxury." I also saw how coming from nothing she was still able to have a good life.

⌘

All the Beautiful Memories

Berenise Lopez

MEXICO

We began the interview at our dining room table and ended up on our porch because my mother wanted to really reminisce on her childhood and her culture. My mother was born and raised in Mexico up until the age of 22, when she decided to relocate to the USA. As she was reminiscing on her childhood and memories of her hometown she became a little emotional, in a good way, because of "all the beautiful memories" she had back in Mexico.

> My house was very small. My father built it with his friends, and that created beautiful memories for me. Growing up there was no such thing as Barbie dolls for my sisters and me. Our dolls were rag dolls we used to make with extra pieces of cloth my mother had lying around. My mother would sometimes help us, which is when the dolls would come out the best.

Usually before the age of 10, girls already knew how to cook, clean the house and help their mothers wash laundry. Young boys would already knew how to help their fathers by handling the livestock or farm. Girls would also have to know how to handle livestock. Usually it was a young boy or the father's responsibility, but sometimes girls also had to deal with the livestock. Young girls would have to feed the animals and also milk the cows to have milk to drink or make cheese.

Washing laundry was pretty fun because we would have to go to the local river, which was about half a mile from our house, and wash laundry there and then bring it home to hang the clothes up to dry. The girl would learn how to cook by shadowing her mother in the kitchen learning recipes from her. Cooking was also a special time where a young girl would bond with her mother.

A young girl usually would be considered a young lady when she got her period. Her period signaled that her body was ready to conceive, but usually it wasn't until the age of 16 that young ladies began a family. Yes, 16 was the "normal" age to begin a family.

What did people usually eat?

The food was much fresher due to the fact that we had crops as well as the livestock at our finger tips. Luckily for us we had different kinds of vegetables and a lot of animals, so we could afford to eat meat. When we needed vegetables we would walk over to the crops and cut whatever it was we needed. We also would get whatever animal was needed.

When a pig or goat was slaughtered, everyone knew it was a big deal because those animals were more expensive. The pig would be used for pig skin or "carnitas," which would be braised in hot oil until the meat was tender and the meat would be used for the tamale filling or tacos or even just served with rice and beans. Food definitely brought family and neighbors together.

One of the most interesting parts of the interview was about celebrations and rituals.

When people got together for anything it was a celebration because people would celebrate that they were healthy enough to enjoy each other's company. But growing up the "Day of the Dead" was a very big deal because that's the time when people would celebrate deceased family members. On the day of October 31st a table would be made for the deceased children. The table would consist of some sort of sweet bread, a variety of fruits, glasses of water and flowers and also a candle for every deceased child. On the evening of the 31st the candles would be lit up so that the children would come and enjoy what was on the table for them. On the morning of November 1st the glasses of water would be changed and new candles would be put out for every deceased adult and that same evening the candles would be lit so the adults can come and enjoy their offerings. In the morning of November 2nd, the table would be cleared and the family usually visited their loved ones' grave site.

A big celebration was also "Three Kings Day," which is celebrated on January 6th. Families and neighbors would gather together to enjoy a special kind of bread with coffee. One had to be careful when eating the bread because it contained small plastic toys inside. Whoever was the "1ucky" one to receive a toy would be responsible for making tamales or a special dish for the people on February 2nd.

Life was clearly different for my mother when she first got to the States. She had lost a lot. Not only was she not used to all the processed foods, but she also didn't have a lot of friends that would celebrate the same holidays she was used to back home.

I learned things from my mother that I didn't know about before – like the "Day of the Dead" – because I had never asked her before. And she appreciated the fact that I interviewed her and cared to know more about how she was raised and her beautiful memories.

⌘

"Jamaica People Need fi Wake Up and Smell the Coffee"

Monique Hewitt-Ramdene

JAMAICA

One of the best ways to learn is through asking questions. In this project, I interviewed Ingrid, a 51-year-old Jamaican mother of three children who was a shopkeeper in her small community. I also drew on some of my own memories of stories told me by my grandparents.

Ingrid lived in a two-bedroom house with her parents and seven siblings. Only the older child gets new clothing, everyone else wears whatever the previous child outgrew; it doesn't matter what gender or color. For example, if Ingrid outgrew a pink linen pants she got from her sister and now it can fit her small brother Raymond, if it's not torn up, Raymond will now wear it. She had one dress for church and one uniform for school. Both were always clean and well steam ironed by her mom's clothes iron that she heats up using a fire. She had old clothing she wore around the yard (judging clothes). Any torn clothing was repaired by her mom with needle and thread.

Her father was a community butcher and a farmer, so they were never hungry. They mostly consumed fresh fruits and vegetables. Whatever produce was in season, that's what they ate. Her father shared his crops with neighbors and the neighbors shared with them in return. Her father raised animals on his farm. Every morning he would milk the cow so her mom could make porridge for the children and his coffee.

Water was never wasted, always recycled. They had a huge concrete tank in the back of the yard which collected rain water and barrels on either side of the house that collected rain water from the gutters attached to the roof. From this water her mother would prepare meals and they would take showers. After taking showers, that water was used to clean the flooring of the house or water the flower garden (if the water is not too soapy). That water was also used to do laundry in a washing pan with a hand brush and then hang on a rope to dry by the wind and the sun.

They didn't have a refrigerator but there was a natural way to preserve food. Her dad would dig a hole in the back of the yard under a big shady tree and food could be stored in that hole for few days. Since her dad was a butcher they had fresh meat all the time. The mom would cook just enough for the day; that way they wouldn't have left overs, and nothing would go to waste. The peels from yam, potatoes, bananas, etc. would feed the pigs.

The ice-cream bike from a neighboring community would come on Sundays after church. Every child waits for that since they only get a treat once every week.

Walking was the main means of transportation. They even walked up to an hour back and forth to visit an ill family member. They had a donkey, but he was only used for transporting produce and other heavy stuff. One of her older brother made a hand cart that was use on the farm to transport fertilizer and hand tools.

There was almost no waste. Everything was repaired or recycle. If it didn't serve one purpose they would create a way to use it for something else. They was no extra food to become waste, bones were fed to cats and dogs, and torn clothing was used to make rugs. They didn't have disposable plastic bags, no bread bags since they made their own bread, no milk cartons because they got milk straight from the cow in their milk buckets.

Children created their own toys. Girls made dolls from old pillow cases and old clothing. Boys made balls from newspapers. They used rubber bands to make Chinese skips (a kind of jump rope) and played hop scotch. The old rope that their father used to tie out the goats was now used by the girls to play jump rope. They played make believe kitchen, they pretended to be school teacher and children, they pretended to be pastors and congregation.

Children looked forward to leisure time because it was family time. They created fun things to do with each other, sometimes so simple but those are the moments they cherished because it was done with family members. They would go to the ponds together to swim. They would go to the forest together looking at different birds and other animals. They would read the Bible together. Their parents would tell them Anansi stories and stories about ghosts.

The older generation passed knowledge to the new generation. The older generation looked out for the children in the community and guided the youngsters on the right path when they were on the street. The younger generation looked up to the older generation as role models. They were very mannerable: 'Yes miss, yes sir, please, thank you, I'm sorry, etc." Young kids helped the elderly carry their bags and buckets. They genuinely cared for each other.

Things and times have sure changed. The way of life is different and the population size has changed. They have five- and six-bedroom houses now made of concrete, each with electricity, electrical appliances of all kinds, running water, and privately owned cars. Kids don't even play with creative toys – they use tablets and cellular phones.

Today the way of life in Jamaica is not sustainable. The system – the people, the landscape, the physical world, the climate, the economy, the culture – has changed drastically. I ask myself if it's too late for sustainability. I'm not sure if what's holding us back is denial or ignorance, but we need to respond and the time to do it is now. We need to strengthen community roots and culture. The government doesn't seem to care much about sustainability.

I remember this proverb my granny used to say: "Jamaica people need fi wake up and smell the coffee," which means they need to act boldly and quickly to sustain their culture.

⌘

Part Three: Africa and the Mediterranean

Trees Have Been Cut Down to Construct Office Buildings

Lisa Acquan

GHANA

I conducted an interview with my 69-year-old grandfather to talk about life growing up in West Africa, Ghana. He was watching the news when I inquired if I could ask him a few questions about his life before he moved to Canada, his permanent home.

When he turned ten years old, my grandfather went to live in a big town called Kumasi with his uncle, who raised him and paid off his school expenses. His mother, my great grandmother, could not afford to send him to school, and his father, a traditional priest, was not a responsible father.

His uncle was very a successful man so he had a few cars and a big house compound in a very beautiful neighborhood. Since his uncle was rich, my grandfather did not lack anything. He had about five decent pairs of sandals that he wore to school, and his uniforms were not torn like those of other children he went to school with. He ate three meals a day and sometimes used to share his meal with his best friend, who came from a home where it was hard to get a decent meal to eat.

Most people, both young and old, who did not have cars usually rode bicycles to get places. When my grandfather turned 15, his uncle bought him his first bicycle so he did not have to take the bus to school. Luckily, Ghana has only wet and dry seasons, so they do not experience winter like here in America.

His uncle had a couple of farms where they planted stuff like plantains, yam, onions or tomatoes. They had an air-ventilated storage room for food. Because of the farm they always ate fresh food grown without fertilizers. The soil was really good, unlike what we're used to in our generation. Today they use fertilizers and other drugs to make the food grow faster.

Grandfather said that when he was growing up, the environment was much cleaner and there was less pollution than in our environment today. Since they did not have many cars in the town at the time, there wasn't much air pollution. The rivers were much cleaner then, and the weather wasn't as hot.

When my grandfather graduated from college, he got a free scholarship to work for an oil company in Canada, and that's where he spent most of his life. Many years after he left the country he went back to visit his family and he realized that the country has changed considerably. It has improved (in one sense) with more technology and more schools than before. Lots of people drive now and fewer people ride bicycles. But a lot of the trees have been cut down to build office buildings. Though he understood the point of all the changes – to create more jobs for the people – he missed how peaceful and quiet the town used to be, especially at night. Now it is more crowded and always noisy. He would never trade his memories of the Ghana of his childhood.

⌘

Grandma's "Wonder Oven"

Sandra Ghatas

EGYPT

My grandmother has always loved cooking and I must admit that her dishes are quite savory! When we were growing up, my parents made it a tradition to ensure that we spent at least a week at my grandparents' place because we lived far away from one another. My siblings would look forward to summer holidays because we knew we would be spoilt by grandma's treats, which I must say I miss quite a lot as an adult.

I vividly recall a conversation I had with my grandmother two years ago to gather some insights about her life and culinary experiences "back in the day" when we did not have microwaves and instant kitchen gadgets as we know them today. As usual, she was excited to talk about matters related to food, as she loved the kitchen and cooking was a hobby to her.

As we chatted along, she made jokes as to how she made sure that her husband always had his food hot and tasty any time of day and night. She took pride in this fact.

> Oh darling, I remember my days as a newly married wife after our wedding and how your grandfather would say nice things to me about how I was the best wife anyone would wish for! The best part was when he would beam in delight as I'd serve his vegetable, rice and beef stew steaming hot any time of day and night, ... and you know how Grandpa is particular about his food.

That statement sparked off some curiosity in me and I was keen to find out how she did this, knowing very well that seventy years ago there were no microwaves in the little town in Egypt where they lived. It is important to mention that my grandfather, who is now ninety years old, would leave the house before dawn to travel 25 miles to work, and he would come home late, sometimes even past midnight, when the workload was high. My grandmother, two years younger and with a limited education, had actually married my grandfather with the hope of a better life. It was important to her then, that she always had hot food for him when he arrived at whatever time of the night.

Grandma told me about what she called a "wonder oven," or what is termed a fireless cooker. It is basically used to ensure that food remains hot over a very long period of time.

> I would cook dinner at around 4pm, and after serving a portion for the kids, I would place your grandfather's food in this wonder oven and cover it nicely, and he would always get it hot, much to his glee, whatever time he came home.

The "wonder oven" was a basket with insulation material, usually hay, placed between the basket and the lining material, which was then sewn all around the basket to keep the insulation in place. A compact cushion would be made from both hay and sponge to cover the basket at the top. This would ensure that the fireless cooker would retain heat as long as it was not opened unnecessarily.

For items such as rice, she did not have to wait until it was completely cooked. As soon as it started boiling, she would get it out of the stove and into the basket and it would continue cooking using the heat that's captured by the insulating material (the hay, in this case).

FIRELESS COOKERS SIMILAR TO GRANDMA'S "WONDER OVEN"

This, in my opinion, was quite an energy saver and I think that we can adopt it in our kitchens today as a form of sustainable technology.

⌘

There's Always Time for a Mint-Flavored Red Tea Under a Fig Tree

Lida Abu Khader

ERMIMEEN, JORDAN

For this paper I interviewed my mother, Nour Sayegh, who grew up in Jordan but later moved to the United States as a young teenager and lived here until her early twenties. I am now writing her story in this narrative of her life. Currently, because we are not in the same country, I am asking my mother the questions through Skype. But whether it's on the phone or face-to-face, my mother paints a bright image of her memories that makes me feel as if I was right there with her.

Her story begins in a small village in Jordan, 20 km east of the capital Amman. My mother was born during a blossoming green spring and named Nour after the holy day in which she was born, what we call here 'Holy Saturday,' but in Arabic it translates to "light."

In this village, Ermimeen, they are all related or at least know each other by name. My mother remembers her village not having electricity. She recalls the day when they first got a fridge; it was an event for them and for other people in the town. She tells a story about how one day an old lady visited them and put her shoes in the fridge thinking it was a cabinet. That was how simple people were back in those days.

People lived a simple life back home. Everything they ate was freshly grown in their orchards and gardens. Bread was baked every morning, before the sun woke everyone up, by her mother on a special brick oven designed for bread. All things were from the season: watermelons, figs, and pomegranate in the summer; leafy greens in the fall; lemons and oranges in the winter; and green cherries and apples in the spring. Everyone was satisfied with what they had, shared their meals, and always made time for a hot mint flavored red tea under a fig tree.

As she grew, many Christian families in her town started to move to the States, and her family was one of them. So when she was in the 8th grade she joined her siblings in their departure to the United States, leaving behind so many beautiful memories. Here in Yonkers, NY, they faced a new life together with many obstacles; a different culture, community, habits, country, policy, and a new language.

Her brothers were strict. They didn't allow her to go to birthday parties or hangouts with her friends. American society viewed her in a new way, judged her for not having a boyfriend and having different values. Though she wasn't allowed a boyfriend or dating, she realized she would look into this subject of gender mixing when she reached the proper age for marriage.

When my mother sees me or my siblings relying so much on our smart phones, she tells us how she encountered a different lifestyle. For instance, she would communicate with her friends by reflecting the mirrors off of the sun after school to signal to each other that it was play time. They would invent games, like placing a long ledge of wood over a rock to play see-saw. Her time was very different than ours.

> Do you think I played with my phone 24/7 when I was your age? No! I used to get dirty and play outside, run around and learn things.

Now fast forward a lot of years to me living in Yonkers, where my mom used to live, and studying here at Westchester Community College. I am proud that I'm doing this assignment for this anthropology class so that I can share my mom's experience and memories and her life story.

⌘

PART FOUR: IRAN

When I Was a Kid

Davoud Tehrani

TEHRAN, IRAN

What follows are my experiences and those of my close relatives in Iran when we were still children. I come from a lower middle class setting in Tehran, the capital of Iran. My parents, two brothers, and I lived in a house with two big rooms. My four older sisters had already married and lived with their husbands. Though the house was relatively large, with a big backyard, we had only one closet for the whole family to hang our clothes.

My family did not own many shoes either. I vividly remember taking my newly purchased shoes to the shoe repair store to attach *naal*, small metal pieces shaped like horseshoes, to the soles at both front and back so that they would not be worn out easily. The whole shoe was made of genuine leather. Once a week I would shine my shoes. One of my well-to-do nieces also reported that her parents, upon purchasing her shoes, would ask the shoemaker to attach a piece of rubber to the heels of her shoes.

My eldest sister made clothes, including underwear, for her six kids herself. "People did not throw things away. That was not the custom, whether you were rich or poor," she said. "How could you not value something that you have made with your own hands?" she reflected, referring to how nothing makes the new generation happy for long. She used to weave socks, gloves, hats, and scarves, and she made tablecloths and pillowcases that she decorated with needlework.

Students' jackets had a removable white cloth sewn on the collar so that the jacket would not get dirty or worn out. That cloth was removed and washed weekly.

When I was a kid, we would shop every day. Many families, including my married sisters, would keep their food cool the natural way in *paasheers* during the summer because we didn't have refrigerators. The *paasheer* worked like this: in the old days city people would build a big underground reservoir to store water. Stairs led to a faucet far below ground level where people got their cooking and drinking water. The faucet in Farsi is called *sheer*, and *paa* is foot, so *paasheer* is the place where the faucet is located. The *paasheer* is quite cool during the summer.

The summer was not as hot in Tehran as it became later. We did not have air conditioners or fans. If we did not go to the countryside, we used to sleep, like many people, in the backyard or on the rooftop during the summer. It was very pleasant and fun. In the evening, people usually would sprinkle water over their yards and bushes to cool off the home.

The weather has always been very hot in the summer in Yazd, however, a city in the desert in southern Iran. They used a very old cooling system that's also found in Egypt and India, the *baad gir* (literally, wind catcher). This is a structure that looks a little like a chimney with openings near the top on one or more sides, an upright tunnel that caught the wind and brought it through the house. Some wind catchers are designed to pull the air over cool water before it enters the house and exits through the tower.

When I was little, we would bathe once a week at the public bath. My friend Javad commented on the custom of weekly bathing only on Friday (the day off): "We didn't recognize the smell of perspiration; we were used to it." However, later on I bought a barrel, painted it black, and installed it on the roof of our spare kitchen located at the other end of the yard. I made a hole through the ceiling and ran a pipe and connected a shower head. I would fill the barrel with water with a rubber hose, and (except in the winter) I could take showers with warm water.

Cold weather was more of an issue in Tehran than hot weather. In winter we kept ourselves warm, especially at night, by using a *korsi*, a low square table covered with big quilts, with mattresses laid on all four sides. There were also upright cushions on the sides where they could lean against the wall of the room. People in the winter sat on the mattresses during the day or in the evenings. They used to eat their dinners on top of the *korsi* and then sleep under the covers. The *korsi* was heated by charcoal embers.

In those days, there were very few cars and people mostly walked, used bicycles, or took buses. There were also horse-drawn carriages to take people all over the city. Aside from that there were donkey-drawn carts that would carry foodstuffs and other materials. My older sister remembers streetcars in downtown Tehran. However, later on the government replaced them with buses. By the time I was ready to go to high school, I went to school by bus. Later I bought a bicycle like my brothers, who used to commute with their bicycles to work.

In the old days, there were no garbage trucks, and as I remember, the garbage of the whole side street of maybe 25 families was not more than could fit in a one-man pushcart.

There were no plastic bags, no food wastes, no cans, no packaging in the daily garbage pile. When I bought yogurt or milk, I would take our own bowl to the store. We would take our own tote bags to purchase rice, beans, etc. Bread and produce were purchased unwrapped or wrapped in newspaper.

It was unimaginable for people to leave their furniture on the sidewalk for garbage collectors to crush like they do in New York City. No one would throw away things that could somehow still be reused or fixed. My sister told me that when they used to make sheets, the excess cloth was used as rags in the kitchen or for making dolls or cleaning shoes, etc. When they bought slaughtered chickens from the market, they would use the feathers to stuff pillows. Vendors went from one neighborhood to another shouting, "I fix broken plates, pots, and teapots." Cars, especially American and German ones, were durable and made to last a lifetime; people kept them for as long as they could. They painted them, repaired the engines, fixed inside and outside. There were no complicated computer parts in cars. Most men could fix their own cars.

When I was a child, I did not have any toys to play with except the ones I created myself. Once I made a movie projector out of a cardboard box and a magnifying glass. Another time one of my nieces and I made shoes out of cardboard and paper. My niece and her older sister made make-believe grocery stores and their parents would shop from them, and I made a make-believe greeting card store (my father had a book and greeting card store). My older brother and one of my nephews made scooters out of wood and old car bearings. Later on, when I bought a small bicycle, I decorated it and wrapped the metal bars with plastic ribbons so the bars would not get damaged. Once I made a small cabinet with two drawers for my belongings.

One of my older sisters, too, remembers making her own dolls and toys and making toy tables and chairs with carpenters' wastes. My nieces made their own dolls, toy mattresses, blankets, and pillows. They made different foods in small portions in their make-believe kitchen in the backyard. One of my nephews described how he and his brothers used to make parking garages with matchsticks. They would drive the matchbox around, in and out of the garage, as if it were a car, all the while making car engine noises. They played with walnuts, marbles, small stones, unusable bicycle wheels, etc. *Ye ghol do ghol*, played with five small stones (similar to the American game of jacks), was a popular game. When my parents later bought me a small toy locomotive, I played with it all the time.

It is important to mention that, with a less luxurious life, there was sufficient leisure time left for our family to do fun things. We would go out of town with other relatives for three months every summer to a village next to a river and beautiful tall mountains, a place with many trees and springs. My brother-in-law owned land there and loved to share his place with other relatives, sometimes as many as 50-60 people. Today it's a two-hour commute by car from Tehran, but then it took us one day to reach our destination. First, we would ride on a bus or minibus to the dirt road leading to the village. From there we would ride on donkeys, which would take up most of the day. This was one of the most fun things: kids riding on donkeys and racing.

At times, my father would close his store and join us for a week or two. My father had enough income to secure the household needs and essentials; therefore, he did not need to work all summer.

Every day while we were in the countryside, we kids used to make a dam in the nearby river and swim, hike trails, explore all the surrounding areas (which had no walls or fences), play volleyball and ping pong (on a ping pong table that took me more than a week to build from scratch out of branches), etc. They grew all kinds of fruits and vegetables on that land. We used to get our daily water from the nearby spring. The kids would make miniature mud houses, with yards and pools with fountains, and when we finished our projects, the grown-ups would choose a winner and grant a prize. We sometimes put on a play that we had written ourselves. At the end of the summer when we had to leave to begin school, kids in unison would sadly say goodbye to the mountains, the river, the spring, etc.

When I still was a small boy, there was a big wooded area of about 4-5 square miles near our house. In the evening there seemed to be millions of noisy crows returning home to the wooded area from all over the city. There were many such cool wooded areas in and around the city and on Fridays (the weekend in Iran) people would have picnics in them. The summer was mostly cool and pleasant, especially in the neighborhoods in the foothills, closer to the mountains.

The sky was crystal clear and filled with stars at night. The Alborz mountain range could be seen from all around the city. In the winter the mountains were covered with snow, and Tehran usually got 2-3 feet of snow, too. Everywhere in the city there was running water in the *joobs* rushing down from the Alborz Mountains. There were many *qanats* (aqueducts) in the city and plenty of underground water. There was also clear water running in *joobs* (open street canals), which some nights would feed the underground storage depots or reservoirs of every house in the neighborhood. That was the household's drinking water.

Now Tehran is one of the most polluted cities in the world. The Alborz mountain range is always hidden in the smog. People celebrate if one day – because of precipitation or strong winds – they can have a glimpse of the mountains, but they also know that the clear sky will last only for one day or maybe just a few hours. Some days the government has to close elementary schools and ask the elderly and people with heath conditions to stay home. There is hardly any snow in Tehran.

There are millions of cars in the city. With the bad quality of gasoline, mass-produced cars that don't meet modern international emission standards are the main source of carbon monoxide, particulate matter, and hazardous fumes. In addition to the locally generated pollution, in recent years there has been a kind of hazardous dust coming from the west, both from Iraq and from the western part of Iran, where dams and misuse of water have caused drought and dried up several lakes.

By the time I finished high school, cars were everywhere. Durable and expensive European and American cars gave way to cheap, domestically assembled cars. The wooded area in our neighborhood was divided into small lots for building construction. All the trees were cut down and the birds lost their homes.

Under the pressure of "modern" life, we moved northward into an apartment in a more middle-class district. My brother, my father's partner at that time, expanded the business and my father went into debt. The facial expression of a happy father increasingly turned into the grim look of a man always preoccupied with huge debt, not knowing how to pay it off.

When I was small, there were only a million people living in Tehran and about 15 million in the whole country. Most of the population lived in self-sufficient villages. Since then, villagers have increasingly been migrating to the cities and the population of the country as a whole has quadrupled as well. Tehran's population grew from 1 million in 1950 to 8.7 million in 2018. Builders started to construct cheap, flimsy apartments across the rapidly growing city. In a recent visit to my birthplace downtown, I could not even recognize the neighborhood and I was practically lost. Two-thirds of the side streets where we used to live and where kids used to play have turned into big throughways. Our house, with its big backyard and trees, has been replaced with a five-story apartment building. The same thing happened with all the other houses in our street. I could not detect even one tree in the whole neighborhood. Now, on my eldest sister's street in northern Tehran, a hilly area that used to have one-family houses on large lots, there is nowhere to park. Most of the one-story houses have turned into big apartment buildings, full of families that each own at least two cars.

If there's a silver lining to this story, it would be that it's all happened so fast that millions of people have experienced the change and the loss and are all looking for solutions.

⌘

Cool Water and Wind Catchers

*Ali Hodavan, with Bahman Bazargani**

Two friends and I sat drinking tea on the porch of a villa in Damavand, a town on the slopes of Mount Damavand, the highest peak in Iran and the highest volcano in Asia. We mostly talked about ways we used to keep cool in the summer and how we kept foodstuffs cool and preserved them for year-round use in the old days.

Ali worked for years in Sistaan, a province in the south east of Iran, teaching English. Now he has retired and lives in Tehran. Bahman grew up in the northwest, in Tabriz, but now he lives in Tehran and Damavand.

Ali explained that in Sistaan, a desert province, there's a very strong 120-day wind during the summer that people used to

---

* This and all the following interviews in this section were conducted by Davoud Tehrani in Iran.

cool off their houses with some very elementary methods. They made channels from the roof into the house [wind tunnels, wind chimneys] that would catch the wind and send it down into the house. At the top they put rough textured straw or other weeds and a tap to wet them with water. The wind would go through the wet straw and cool off before blowing down into the house. They called these *khaarkhaane*, or house of straw. Air conditioners in Tehran use the same principle, except they use electric fans to pull the air through the straw and into the house. The *khaarkhaane* is a more modern version of the traditional *baad gir* or wind catcher of Kashan and Yazd.

WINDCATCHERS ON HISTORIC BUILDING IN KASHAN, IRAN

Though he worked for many years in Sistaan, Ali grew up in Tehran. "There was a little pool in the cellar of our house and that water was cold," Ali said. "We would put our pickles and jam jars in that pool." Then he smiled, remembering how they would take water from big springs and big *qanats* (underground aqueducts), and how some vendors would fill a big tank on a horse-drawn wagon with water and go around the neighborhoods to sell it to people. This was in the center of the city called Aab-e-Shah (king's water) in Arg Square.

SHESH BADGIRI RESERVOIR OF YAZD, IRAN. WATER IN THE AAB ANBAR IS COOLED BY SIX WINDCATCHER TOWERS. (PHOTO © BORNA_MIR / ADOBE STOCK)

People also dug wells. There was plenty water in Tehran. There were also big *aab anbars* (underground reservoirs) for public use, like *Aab anbarha-ye Shah Abbasi*, built by a shah, or king, who lived about 500 years ago. Actually there were lots of public *aab anbars* named Shah Abbasi, in several big cities.

Houses had *aab anbars*, too, and they would put *sang-e-namak* (rock salt) and also fish in them to

111

purify the water. In Shemran there was so much water running that people couldn't sleep at night (because of the sound).

In the old times when people did not have a refrigerator, they would come up with many ways to keep food. For example, I remember in Tehran throughout the winter we would keep our meat in a hole dug in the snow pile in the flower garden (we would gather all the snow from the rooftop and drop it in the yard. And there were people in our street that would shout *"barf paroo meekonim"* (we shovel snow).

Where Bahman grew up, in Tabriz, a northeastern province of Iran, it was colder than Tehran. At the beginning of winter, he explained, people used to butcher 2-3 fattened up sheep, *gusfand-e-parvar*, skin them and put them in big pots called *gaazaan*. They would cook them in the *gaazaan* with the fat of the tail of the sheep. Then they would dig a hole in the basement and bury them. They would pour the fat over the top of the meat and then pile clay dirt on top of it and that would keep the meat all winter.

It's quite remarkable that all three of us, born during or just after World War II, clearly remember a time when we could keep cool or warm, get a drink of cold water, and even preserve our food without using electricity.

⌘

Good Times

Javad Alavi

QAZVIN

This interview was conducted on a bus to Sareyn in Tabriz province, northwestern Iran. Javad Alavi and some of his many friends periodically rented a bus and travelled to various corners of Iran. While we were going through the mountains, enjoying the view of clear sky and green farms, I asked Javad if I could interview him and his friends on the bus, and he agreed. Javad and I sat next to each other and talked about his childhood memories, starting with his father.

> My father was a trader (*taajer*) of raisins, dates and textiles. He would bring all these items from Moscow or Baku.

"Did he import charcoal for the household from Russia, too?" I joked.

"We had charcoal," he laughed. But that reminded him of the *korsi*.

Actually, this is interesting. You may not know since you lived in Tehran when you were a child. At the beginning of Shahrivar (September), people made *garde zoghal* (charcoal powder) into balls 6 inches in diameter with water. Then, we would cut the ball in half and add embers from an outside fire into it. [Embers were used after they had finished burning and were not smoking.] This way the balls became red hot inside. We would put that charcoal all in a metal container and cover it with ashes and then put that inside the *korsi*, with ashes on top. It smolders, slowly giving off heat.

"We did the same thing," I said.

Our kitchen was under most of the house and on top of the basement (cellar). We had something made from boards, 2 by 3 meters, that would hang from the basement ceiling and it had food in it. [This seems to be to protect the food from animals.] Basements were very cool in the summer.

Water was kept in an *aab anbaar* (underground reservoir) in the house for cooking and drinking and it was cool. There were 50-100 steps down to the place where water was kept. [This seems like an exaggeration—20 is more like it] The *aab anbaar* is made of bricks and because the bricks absorb water, the water was always cold. They fed the *aab anbaar* from a *qanat* (underground aqueduct) that was coming from outside the city. It was usually done after midnight.

During the day, the water was running in surface canals and was used by people for watering gardens, etc. Someone would open the channel at night when the water was clean and fill the *aab anbaar*. There was a faucet to get drinking water at the bottom of the stairs.

The *aab anbaar* had a bad smell. Some people put rock salt into the *aab anbaar*, and some people put fish in it—all to kill the smell. It was dark in there. If it was not filled with fresh water for a long time the water smelled, too.

I asked him what kinds of toys he had or if there were any games in Qazvin that I did not play in my childhood in Tehran.

Okay. We played with walnuts and marbles. There was a game called *anovah*. You had to go to a high place so your friends couldn't grab you [a form of tag]. We would make a hole in an empty can and attach a string and drag it. It would make a noise and we would pretend that we were driving a car.

"Kids in Tehran did the same things," I said. It turns out he even made an *aapaarat* (movie projector) to show movies just like I did, using a light and a box and a magnifying glass, turning the reel by hand.

The family would all come in the evening and I would show the movies, and my grandmother really liked it, to come to visit "Cinema Javad." She would smoke, since in those days everybody would smoke at the real movies. [Her smoking was a compliment to him because she was acting like it was a real cinema.] She didn't like the real cinema because they showed too much skin, kissing, etc. I showed more innocent movies.

One of the favorite stories I heard in these interviews was Javad's story about a kid playing with a bicycle wheel with no tire on it. The boy was using a stick in the notch to roll the wheel along at high speed, which took some skill. He was pretending to drive a car. Then a small kid asked, "Can I ride along?" The big kid said, "Come aboard" [*bia baalaa*] and took the little kid's hand, and then another little kid asked to "ride." Soon there was a line of kids holding hands running along after the wheel.

"Was it clear in Qazvin in those days who had more money, who had less?" I asked.

> No, it wasn't obvious. Everybody wore the same kind of clothes. Of course, there were groups of people that lived uptown who ironed their trousers and wore *cula ye labedar* (hats with brims). We put metal taps on the toes and heels of our shoes. Poor people would put an extra layer of sole on the shoe when they bought it so it wouldn't wear out.

"What did you do with your excessive stuff?"

> Everything that existed was used. If one of the straws came off of the broom, they would put it back. If they couldn't use the broom any more, they would use it for fuel in the *tanoor* (bread oven). They roasted melon seeds and gave melon peels to horses or sheep. Corn cobs would go for the *tanoor*, too.
>
> I forgot to tell you that we made a dam in the river and the water would build up and we would swim in the water. There was a belief among people if you pee in the water, all around you the water would turn blue [so everyone would know

what you did], and this was the reason why nobody peed in the water.

"Tell me about human relations."

Relationships were traditional. Nobody would invite each other to their houses. At the door they would shout: "Mash Qasem [he just made up a name], are you home? I'm coming in." That was how they would go to each other's houses. That's how they did it. At night, nobody was alone. They would go to each other's houses. Usually the extended family got together every night, but taking turns, this sister-in-law or that sister-in-law.

⌘

Rowboats to the Sea

Parvaane Aalebuye

The next person interviewed on the bus tour was Parvaaneh, a retired literature teacher from Langerood, in the northern part of Iran near the Caspian Sea. Her father had been a *maalek* (landowner) and worked in the mayor's office.

Parvaaneh's family had fruit trees in the backyard and grew vegetables. They shopped for food every day and used to keep food in a basket hanging in the well because it was cool.

Langerood was mostly self-sufficient in food. Whatever they didn't have in the town, such as wheat, was brought in by river from the Caspian Sea.

Children in Langerood had fun running around the rice fields on the dikes of the paddies after they harvested rice, when the paddies were dry. She said it was fun because you try not to fall.

We played with the animals, too. In the summer we went away for three months to a place near the sea, as our summer vacation.

Twice a year – in September and March, the beginning of school year and at new year (spring) – they bought fabrics and either their mother or the tailor would make clothes.

"We wore those clothes until they got holes in them," she laughed.

More or less everybody dressed pretty much like each other and there wasn't much difference. When children were coming [to school] from the villages, even then we all dressed the same.

I want to tell you a story from the time when I was in 11th grade. At that time, nobody would wear *gaalesh* [cheap plastic or rubber shoes]. But one time, a village girl came to school wearing *gaalesh*. We kids all bought gaalesh and wore them to school so that she wouldn't be embarrassed. However, my mother didn't like it.

At that time, *aks-bargardun* (image-transfers) was a fad so we decorated our *gaalesh* with them.

Some of Parvaane's favorite memories had to do with her youth and the river that ran to the Caspian Sea.

In that life we had more relationships and more freedom outside of the house. That was empowering. Now technology is giving us power – but we had other kinds of power. We wrestled, boys and girls, it didn't matter. Life was simpler. They [the parents] trusted us.

Now it's hard to get to know each other. Today's kids don't have the kind of relationships that we

120

used to have. In those days, we had closeness and openness and people really liked each other.

The river that connected our town to the sea was itself so much fun. We all, boys and girls, with all our brothers and cousins, got onto rowboats, like a carnival. Fifteen boats, each with a *faanus* (oil lamp).

Everyone had a musical instrument. They played flute, drums. We sang until we got to the mouth of the river at the sea. Lovers sang love songs. We had norms to follow and nobody would disregard those norms. Everybody was watching themselves.

And now the river hasn't much water, and it's polluted, too.

⌘

They Throw Away Food Enough for Fifty People!

Mehrdad

SAREYN

When the bus tour reached our destination, we stayed in a hotel in Sareyn, Ardebil province of northern Iran. I walked around in the town looking for someone to interview. Eventually I found an older guy (born 1949) sitting on a stool next to a car repair shop. Like most people I asked, he was more than happy to be interviewed about his childhood experiences. We started with the weather, since Sareyn is one of the coldest areas in the country. A lot of people go there in the summer to escape the polluted cities and to enjoy the cool weather and the many hot springs that make it a tourist area.

> When I was a child, there was so much snow in the alley that we went from one roof to another. The water in the river was clean. We went into the river and played in the water. The women would go and

bring cool water to the house. This place was full of grass and full of fruit trees. It was like a park.

Now the river, the same river that ran the flour mill, has dried up and we are faced with not much water around here.

There used to be a lot of our local breed of *gaavmish* (very large cows). Now there are very few of them.

And we warmed up our house with *tanoor* (an underground clay oven for baking bread) and *korsi*, which we set up over the *tanoor*. When the smoke of the *tanoor* had finished, we would cover the last burning part with ashes [*hapskardan*]. We cooked with the *tanoor*, both tea and stew meat, which we put in a pot and lowered into the *tanoor*. For the fire, we used either wood or dried cow pies. In the room, there were a number of holes to let the smoke go outside.

He talked about clothing and social relationships.

Clothes were made of wool, by women. Landlords wore two pairs of shoes, one regular shoe and then a rubber shoe over it. One peasant noticed that and followed the landlord and the landlord asked, "Why are you following me?" The peasant answered, "Everybody wears one pair of shoes. Why are you wearing two?"

In another incident, a peasant was watering trees by opening up the irrigation ditch with his shovel. His pants legs were rolled up and I told him to roll them back down to his ankles because he would scratch and injure his skin with the shovel. He said, "Then my pants will get a hole and where will I get another pair of pants?"

Our community relations were very close: rich and the poor. *Arbabs* (landlords), *khans* (chiefs), all of them were close (*samimi budan*). People were helping each other. Everybody used to go to visit each other's houses a lot. Now if you go somewhere twice, they say, "Oh, you were here last night."

We played with the sheep (chasing them, riding on them, etc.). Also, we played with sheep bones. We played on the ice. We played with sticks and branches.

We got our food right from here. We had all the meat here. However they brought beets, sugar and cube sugar from Ardebil (the closest city). People were self-sufficient. There were little stores, too. They had a flour mill run by water power. In the beginning of the fall they would bring the wheat to the mill and make flour for the winter. Every day we baked bread in the *tanoor*, and that warmed the house too.

When asked to compare the past and modern times, Mehrdad had strong opinions.

In my opinion, those days were good. That was the real life. That was life. *Aabgusht* (a stew made with meat, potatoes, and beans) was delicious. Spoons for eating it were made of wood.

Now there's a lot of everything. Now during the fasting days, they give a public dinner for breaking the fast and afterwards they throw away food enough for fifty people!

Now we use gas, which doesn't have smoke. That's good. Back then, there was one lantern that we used to do everything: make a carpet, cook food. Now when they turn on 30 lights, people still say, "It's dark." I tell them, "Kids, in those days we used one light to do everything." The kids say, "You're cheap" [meaning you don't want to pay a high electricity bill].

⌘

Now There's Everything, But No Happiness

Seyyed Mohammed Hoseini and Agha Kordebache

Some of the most beautiful places in the world are villages on the slopes of the Alborz mountain range not far from Tehran. We used to spend our summers in the village of Aghasht, and we still sometimes visit other villages in the region.

Seyyed Mohammed was born in 1936 in Aghasht. We both enjoy talking about the environment, and he could well remember the past in his home village.

> There was really a lot of water in the river in the past. There was so much water that sometimes we couldn't go in it. The winter would get so cold that sometimes the river would totally freeze and then people had to cut stairs in the ice to get home. And sometimes we had so much snow that we had to shovel the snow twice in 24 hours from the roof. Afterwards, we would go hunting *kapk* [a bird that

puts its head under the snow] and wild goats. The mountains had snow on them until the end of August.

In Sorghehesar, a village between Aghasht and Tehran, I met another old-timer, Mr. Kordebache. He remembered winters with 2-3 meters of snow, when the people made tunnels in the lane to go through.

In the winter, if you wanted to come from Ghalehassankhan (a village two kilometers away from their own village), there were wolves. The cold of the past doesn't exist anymore.

Before they made the Karaj dam and reservoir, the river that was running through the village always had water. The water was clean. We used that water. We filled our clay water pots. Now it's become a sewer. Nobody's conscience allowed him to pollute that water in those days. Nobody peed in the water there, everyone was careful and watching over it. We were all locals. The river ran many kilometers and nobody was doing anything to it. It was so clear that you could count the stones on the bottom.

Now there's not much snow. Back then the snow was so heavy you would have to shovel the snow off your roof 3-4 times in 24 hours.

The thought of all this loss caused Kordebache to sigh and slap his hand on his lap,

Now, there's everything but no happiness.

Speaking of happiness, I asked Seyyed Mohammed about communal ties.

In those days the families and close neighbors would get together in somebody's house. They would sit around the *korsi* and read/recite the *Shahnameh* [an Iranian classic about the ancient kings]. That was fun.

How did they keep food? I asked.

We would choose a sheep and fatten it up to about 60-70 kilograms. One month past the beginning of autumn, we would slaughter it. Then we would cut it into little pieces [*ghormehi*] and cook it in its fat. After that we would fill a big tall clay pot with flour. Then we would add the pieces of meat coated with fat in layers with flour between the layers. Every time that we wanted meat we would take a bunch of pieces and cook it in the fat that it was already coated with.

They did something similar in Sorghehesar, Mr. Kordebache said. After they killed the sheep and cut it in pieces and cooked it in the fat of the tail, they would put the cooked meat in the skin of the sheep to preserve it. Either that or they would put it in the *pastoo* (a cool place in the back of the house), in a huge clay pot and add salt. Then when they wanted to use it, they would dig out the meat with a spoon and take whatever they needed.

In the summer in Aghasht, Seyyed Mohammed explained, people would use fresh meat every day. Neighbors took turns killing an animal and sharing with the others so meat would get eaten and never go bad.

Houses were made of *khesht* [mud bricks]. The walls were 50cm thick! On the outside of the walls they would smear mud mixed with straw to keep out the cold in the winter and the heat in the summer. The entrance door was small so that the cold couldn't get in.

Under every house was a place for the sheep. Everybody had that. Women would take care of the sheep and animals. They milked them. Week by week the milk would be shared around among the neighbors, because we would have extra milk and shared it with others, and they would do the same thing. From the sheep's milk they would make cream and butter and ghee (clarified butter).

At the beginning of spring, on the New Year, the elders of the village would start going from house to house from the beginning of the village to end, visiting every house. It would take three days. After that [on the 4th day of the New Year], everyone [the men] went up onto the roof of the mosque and put out carpets and sat on them. Ten people who were *sarbune* [family heads] would explain the laws [of the village], for example, that the sheep shouldn't go below a particular *joob* [irrigation channel] to graze.

On the roof of the mosque they would ask, "Who wants to become a shepherd?" Somebody would volunteer and people would hire him. For each sheep, they would give him 5-6 kilos of wheat.

The village had 50 male cattle that they grazed in the mountains. Four people were [staying up there] watching them. In the beginning of the fall they would bring them down and give them to their owners. They would bring the female cattle to the front of the mosque every day and the cowherd would take them out to graze and brought them back at night to be milked.

It seems they didn't use money much in those days. I asked Seyyed Mohammed how they paid for the public bath.

Everyone who wanted to go to the public bath had to bring 6 kilos wheat and 4 kilos barley, because the *hamaam* used *buteh* [a particular kind of thorny bush] as firewood to heat up the water. This would be for one year, for men. Women would give bread. Three people were running the *hamaam* and they would go around with a tablecloth to the houses to gather the bread.

The barber didn't have a shop. He would just go around the village at 4 o'clock in the morning. His other job was to open the *hamaam*. He also did circumcisions. He also treated wounds (*zaakhmeh sia*).

What did they eat in those old days, I wondered? Seyyed Mohammed's answer surprised me.

There were no trees at the time. [By this he meant fruit trees. Fruit was a luxury.] Everyone was planting wheat and barley. The village was self-sufficient. Just rice was brought from Shomal [the north of Iran]. Meals were mostly meat and dairy products like yogurt, butter, cheese, milk, cream and bread, of course. We would eat rice once a month.

We had so many cattle that we would sell them, too, to people who would come from other villages.

There were some mulberry trees in the village. These were for poor people. It was considered charity [*vakhf*] to let the poor eat from your tree. At the New Year they would say which tree was for whom.

Were there any special ceremonies, rituals, or games?

All the villagers would go to the cemetery the last Friday of the year. They would make *haleem* [cooked grain and meat porridge]. There were two cemeteries, one for adults and one for kids. They went to the children's cemetery and ate bread and halvah and dates. There was extra bread, which they would give to the unfortunate poor. In addition, they would help the poor at the end of the [fasting] month of Ramadan.

Boys and girls played a game called *alakdolak*. They would lay a short stick on top of two stones, knock it upward with a big stick, then hit it with sticks and if someone catches it their team comes to the base and they are the ones who take the big stick to hit the little stick. [Something like baseball.] There were no toys. We played with the sheep. We could chase them or try to ride on them. They're soft to sit on but then they jump and you fall and everybody would laugh.

What about garbage? I asked.

There was no garbage at all. There was no fruit. Everything from the cow we used. We sold its skin. We used the manure for fuel. The only garbage was walnut shells, which we used to put in the fire. We made use of everything.

We drank water from the river and also from the little streams. They all were clean. Nobody

132

would pollute the water. Everyone was local and they told the kids not to pollute the water because we drink this water. Now there's no culture. People throw garbage anywhere just like that.

Seyyed Mohammed, like many elders interviewed in Iran, thought the present compared unfavorably with the past.

> Everybody was kind to each other, helping each other. If anyone wanted to make a house, everybody would come and help.

> People themselves made the rules at Nowruz (the village meeting at the New Year) and wrote them down, took minutes. Nobody could break those rules because people themselves would ratify those rules and they were present at the meeting. If somebody would break the rules he would have a very hard time.

> In the past, people would elect the *kadkhoda* [village leader] year by year and the *kadkhoda* would be elected the next year if he was good. If they weren't satisfied, they would change him. Everybody would raise their hands to show if they agreed.

> In the evenings, everybody [the men] would go to the teashop and sit there, whether they were poor or rich. You couldn't tell from people's clothes whether they were poor or rich. Everybody used to help each other.

Unfortunately, now the river in Aghasht is just a creek. There is much less snow to feed the river. The musical sound of the water hitting the rocks is gone. Even when there is more water in the springtime you do not hear any sounds because people have taken the rocks to build villas along the river bank. Not only did they steal from the creek but they also polluted it. People threw construction waste like chalk, bits of limestone, etc., next to the creek hoping that the water would somehow, someday wash it all away. It's heartbreaking to see plastic bags and garbage everywhere.

And recently there was a serious flash flood that destroyed the riverbank.

⌘

PART FIVE: EUROPE

Guests Were Constantly In and Out of the House

Sehade Duka

FORMER YUGOSLAVIA

The sweat began to drip down the detailed glass cup filled with Coca Cola placed directly in front of my father on the granite tabletop, the ice quickly melting away. As I was sorting through my paper work, I began to adjust my sweater. I started to feel uncomfortable, as the heaters were set on high. My mother was sitting across from my father, and I was listening. With a smile on his face, my father began to describe the vastly different childhood he experienced in a little village hidden far away in Europe.

My father grew up in a small town (oddly enough) named Spas. It is located in a remote area and a person wouldn't be able to pinpoint it on a map, even with the help of any search engine. He grew up in a small house with only four rooms and an outhouse, with his father, mother, four brothers, and two sisters.

All the surrounding neighbors were relatives in one way or another, either through the wife's or the husband's family. My father explained that it was considered normal for every family to have five or more children to help with the farm work. Families in the area had become accustomed to a noisy and busy home filled with people, considering guests were constantly in and out of the house. With so much free time on their hands and not much to do the adults would gather and drink tea. The children would all get together and run around unsupervised through the entire village. They would often play hide and seek. My father's favorite place to hide was behind the apple trees. Because the children didn't have access to toys, they would create swords with sticks and battle each other to see who would be the victorious knight of the day.

During the summer, all the house doors were left open, and only a sheer piece of cloth blocked the doorways to prevent the sun's heat and bugs from entering the house.

Several times, I myself have visited the house my father grew up in, and I saw a quick change within a ten-year time span. As the years progressed, more and more families started to relocate to live closer to the city. Where the land was once covered with multiple types of apple trees, watermelons, and a vast variety of fruits, all there is now is dead crops.

My father remembers the way he used to live and compares it with how he lives today. He still loves to garden but is limited to a small area in the backyard. He is only able to grow tomatoes, peppers, and cucumbers. He talked about star gazing during the summer nights and being able to see millions of stars in the sky, with the mountains in sight, too. When he looks up at the skies today, his vision is distracted by telephone wires.

From growing up in a four-room house with no indoor bathroom to living in a large house today, my dad has come a long way. Although all my relatives live fairly close, they are not over every day and it's still hard for him to adjust to an empty house. Everywhere we go we have to commute by car, considering nothing is close enough to travel by foot.

During the interview, my father was joking about leaving the house doors open today in the summer and said we would get more than just a cool breeze coming into the house at night. Life has drastically changed for my father and everyday he is still learning to adapt.

⌘

Factories Killed the Soul of our Beautiful Town

Fati Vuillemey

Herve, my husband's older brother, was born 66 years ago in Plancher-bas, a small town in the east of France, not too far from Germany and Switzerland. The town had a population of 1,100 at that time. Herve is convinced that his town is the most beautiful town on earth. This is his story.

> I had two younger brothers. My father, who did not have much education, worked in a French motor vehicle company named Peugeot. Our father was the only one working at the time; my mother was a stay-at-home housewife.
>
> My parents were very strict about our clothes. We must — I mean must — take very good care of our clothing. Our house decor was very simple and humble. In our dining room we had one big heavy

wooden table and four matching wooden chairs, one for each of us.

Our house did not have any air conditioner system; however, we did not get too much sun going into the house, so the temperature inside during summer was pretty cool. We did have one fan, but that could only be used when we were watching TV together in the night when dad was back from his long day of work.

Herve talked about the winters, which were very cold in that old farmhouse.

Winter time was the harshest season for us. Our town is in the mountains, not far from the French Alps, and winter can be really cold. Because our house used to be an old farmhouse, the heating system and the pipes were very old and did not supply enough heat to the entire house. Some nights it was so cold that our mother had to boil four big pots of water and we all gathered in the dining room and let the boiling water warm us through the night.

I used to hate winter. However, I did enjoy the snow because my brothers and I loved playing with our sled made out of plastic from a big barrel. We went to the top of the hill and played until our cheeks got really red. I still miss those old days, where time was invested into valuable activity.

My dad got an old, powerful refrigerator as a reward for his perfect attendance at work. All our perishable foods were stored in the refrigerator. Every month my dad and two of his friends would put money together and buy one big sheep from the farmer who lived five minutes' walk from our house. After slaughtering it, they shared the meat equally. Our share of the meat was packed in small plastic bags and stored in the freezer. My mom used it little by little until the next month. We also had poultry – mostly chickens – in our backyard.

The good thing about Plancher-bas back then is that everybody knew everybody. Families didn't need a babysitter for their children; the neighbors watched the kids. People in the town celebrated good news together and mourned together. Our parents always checked on their elderly neighbors, making sure they had enough food and were warm. As kids our parents never got worried if they did not see us for hours, because they knew where we are. We liked to play at "la place des fetes," the center of the town where there are fireworks on Bastille Day. All children loved to play over there.

The interview continued onto the topics of transportation, garbage, and toys.

People walked most of the time, we did not need much from outside our town. We really didn't see the need of transportation. It didn't seem that we were missing anything of that nature. We got our milk from the farmers, we got a butcher to supply all our meat. Every Friday we had "le marche de Plancher-bas," that is, the market where vendors from outside our town came to sell various goods such as clothing, food, handmade toys, etc.

The time I was growing up we did not have much garbage. Our household trash most of the time was given to our chickens. There is never waste with poultry.

Sometimes we made our own toys. My brother and I liked to play "the mask of Zorro." We made the swords out of branches – it was really fun, and safe, too. Oh boy, I sure miss those days. We had a lot of good free time when I was a kid; one of my favorite play times was when we would go in the woods to hunt for berries. There were so many berry trees in the woods; all the boys of my age enjoyed going into the woods because of the sweet berries. If we didn't go into the woods we would go fishing at the river, which has the biggest trout population in the area. We were never bored as kids. We enjoyed every single day. Life was rich back then. It was not based on how much money, cars or houses you had. It was just about how much you appreciated the things you had and the people who meant a lot to you.

Plancher-bas, like any little town, started changing when some companies bought all our free land so they could build factories to make car parts. That really killed the soul of our town. We started to encounter diseases that we never had before, such as cancer; people started to die at young ages. The farmers started to lose their herds without knowing the cause.

The seasons started to change, too. Climate change is becoming reality. We used to get a good amount of snow, so people could go skiing, but we started to get less and less snow. The level of the river went down a lot and its color also changed. Our berry trees are all gone and there is more open space. We see more big trucks in our small town and have the noise of the trucks and engines. When we started to see new faces in our town, then we really started to feel insecure in our own town.

Talking to my brother-in-law, I thought of how the planet earth is the only place we can call home. If we continue to destroy it, nothing will be left to the generations to come. We have to change our lifestyle.

⌘

In America Everyone Wastes Food Every Day

Fitore Demirovic

FORMER YUGOSLAVIA

On a brisk October morning, I sat with my husband's grandmother and spoke with her about her childhood. She is 89 years old. She comes from former Yugoslavia, where she lived in a small village in the country, far away from any cities.

As we sit together in my living room with cups of hot tea and honey, she tells me about her life. What interested me the most was the differences in the way we got our food. While I have been accustomed to being able to get food whenever I wanted by going to the store, she had to work for everything she ate. Also, I was used to being able to eat many different types of food from around the world. She, on the other hand, ate mostly the same types of food all the time.

All the technology we have today – from food production to transportation and marketing – is all something very foreign to my grandmother-in-law. She got eggs from the chickens in her coop. She got milk from her cows. She made her own cheese from the milk her cows gave. She also farmed her own fruits and vegetables and baked her own bread. To leave her home and arrive in a place where mostly everyone gets their food from someone else, all that she could think was how rich these people must be to be able to get all this food without having to farm or sweat for it.

> My first few weeks here were so confusing. I was wondering how everyone was able to have full fridges and make big dinners every night and it all seemed effortless. I would have to work all day just to put one good meal together and I see it happen here in just a few minutes. And it wasn't just the amount of food, either. It was the variety as well. I was familiar with many fruits and vegetables because we grew them back home, but some foods were so foreign and looked so weird to me that I thought they were just invented.

I told her that although we are lucky today to be able to get food easy and cheap, it is not a sustainable way to produce and consume food. The over-farming is destroying our farmland, the transportation of the food runs on fossil fuels and releases a lot of greenhouse gasses into the atmosphere. I told her that although her way of getting food was physically more difficult, in the end, it was more sustainable. She agreed with this notion.

> Our land was not over farmed, our animals were healthy and not fed with drugs like the farm animals in this country, and also food was not wasted over there, while in America it seems that everyone wastes food every day.

This conversation really put things in perspective for me. It makes me feel both lucky and unlucky for living here in a first world nation. We get all of the comfort and we don't have to worry about going hungry, but the quality of our food has suffered. I can eat a steak whenever I want, but I will not know what meat from a freshly butchered healthy cow tastes like. I can also eat eggs whenever I want, but they will never taste the same as an egg laid the same morning I cooked it. In order to produce all the food we have, factory farms are producing food that might even be dangerous for us to eat, like beef with mad cow disease or chicken with salmonella.

This conversation with my grandmother-in-law taught me that although technology gives people so much, in some ways, it takes away just as much as it gives.

⌘

Older Generations Were Much Smarter About Sustainability

Rosanna Alaimo

CASTRO FILIPPO, AGRIGENTO, SICILY

I decided to interview my grandfather, Salvatore, for this paper because not only is he the oldest member in my family but also because he has so much experience with the way life was in the past.

Grandfather Salvatore was born in Castro Filippo, Agrigento, a fairly small town in Sicily, Italy. He still lives there along with my grandmother and many more relatives. Skype and FaceTime is how we mostly communicate. As I was asking my grandfather some questions, my grandmother also chimed in with her insights about how life used to be.

The way of living was much more sustainable 70-80 years ago than it is today. My grandfather's family didn't have much but they were still content with their lives. My grandmother explained how the women, or housewives, would retrieve water by going to the water canals and filling up large vases. They traveled back home carrying the vases on top of their heads. A majority of the time they would travel to the canals in large groups so more water could be carried back to the house. The last time I went to Sicily, my grandparents took me to the water canals and I experienced "culture shock" seeing how water was once retrieved. I couldn't help thinking to myself how much water we waste.

Our society is utterly obsessed with having more. More televisions, more cars, more clothes, more junk. My grandparents still have the same furniture from when they were married, which was over fifty years ago. Clearly, older generations were much smarter when it comes to sustainability.

⌘

I Eat to Live, I Don't Live to Eat

Noel Pugliese

L'AQUILA, ITALY

Present in the kitchen in Yonkers when I interviewed my 91-year-old Grandfather Lorenzo were hanging peppers, red wine on the table, Catholic crosses, a figurine of a donkey and shepherd, and one energetic grandmother cooking up too many things at once. Aunt Michele joined us after a short while, because what's an Italian life history interview without the whole family chiming in? Grandpa Lorenzo is of full Italian descent, born and raised in the small town of L'Aquila, in central Italy.

The wine was already set on the table. Grandpa Lorenzo starts to help my Grandmother fry up some pizza dough, which they call "pizza frit." According to my grandmother, "everybody loves these. They're like zeppolas but better."

Grandpa, tell me all the things you grow in the garden here in Yonkers, and what did you grow back in Italy?

I have grapes, peppers, parsley, squash, one peach tree, salad, swiss chard, a fig tree, basil, tomatoes – tons of tomatoes, zucchini, and one time a pumpkin by mistake. Back in Italy on my father's farm, we used to have corn, beans, grapes, so many things. We used to do everything by hand, too. I learned how to garden in Italy.

Tell me a little bit about when Uncle Frank goes upstate and hunts.

He would go up and hunt deer along with his son, a few of the cousins, and one time my brother. When he would come back they would butcher the deer and split up the pieces amongst the family. The piece Grandma gets, she would make venison stew.

FUN FACT: When World War 2 was going on in Europe, Grandfather Lorenzo would use German hand grenades to fish in the river. He would take the grenade and detonate it before throwing it in the river in hopes the explosion would kill some fish and float them to the top.

Grandpa, what kind of toys did you have when you were a kid? Did you play anything when you were younger?

I had a bicycle rim with a stick in the middle, and we used to roll it down the street for fun. I had a ball made from a bunch of rags and used to play soccer with that. Soccer was very big in Italy and Europe. Still is.

Grandpa, tell me your most memorable story about the pet donkey you had in Italy.

We used to have cannabis plants by the farm. We used to make what we call "mopine" (towels) out of the plants to clean with. I didn't know at the time what those plants were...

"Yes, you did," interrupted my Aunt Michele. She meant he knew you could smoke the cannabis plants. . . .

No, I didn't!

Anyways, one day we were burning the cannabis plants to refresh the soil, and the donkey was too close to the fumes. Now I know — the donkey got high that day, and ran away from the farm. When I went to go look for her, I found her in the woods near the farm . . . she seemed like one happy donkey.

Grandpa, tell me your most memorable moments with the Germans . . . what do you remember about them?

They came into our village and just took over. They disrespected the women and threatened our survival. They took anything they wanted. One day I hid extra seeds and plants for the farm for next season's planting time. Thank god, they didn't find that stash.

We used to have our livestock and farming up in the mountains in secret spots away from the Germans, so they couldn't take our stuff. The family would take turns going up the mountain to take care of our things.

Grandpa, when you came here, did you find anything about American culture that was odd, or different from yours in Italy?

Where do I begin? One day, me, my mother and father went up to the butcher shop on a Saturday morning. My father told my mother, get whatever

155

you want at the butcher's and cook it. When my mother and I walked into the butcher's, we couldn't believe the amount of food on the counter! In Italy you never had that much! I remember the same for the bars in America, more selection and one dime for one beer.

Grandma comments, "you could have gotten drunk for 50 cents!"

So many women here too. Since I came from a small town in Italy, we never had that many women in one area at a time.

At this, Grandma leans in to listen a little closer.

Grandpa, if you had to choose a phrase, dance, piece of clothing, a food, or a symbol that would represent an Italian, what would it be?

Before Grandpa Lorenzo could even answer, Grandma jokes, "spaghetti and meatballs," and chuckles a little with Grandfather.

Architecture, and yes food.

So, you say architecture. Tell me your favorite building.

The tower of Pisa. Why is it still standing? (We all laugh).

My grandfather has always lived sustainably, back in Italy on the farm and today in Yonkers, where he makes wine for the family from the grapes he grows in the backyard.

Grandpa is very clear about what's important in life, and it's not the endless pursuit of "things." Something he told me a long time ago has just stuck with me all these years: "I eat to live, I don't live to eat."

⌘

The Daredevil Needed a Quick Home Remedy

Adrianna Mendoza

ITALY

After dinner, it was just me and my grandma Raffaelina hanging out in the living room watching an LMN movie we've seen 1,001 times . . . they never get old. I asked her if she was feeling up to answering a couple questions about what they did for medicine back then so I can use it for a project I had due for one of my classes. She replied, "Sure! First, let's go in the kitchen to cut the pound cake and make some espresso in case I fall asleep on you." What a great way to begin my Q and A!

Q: Okay mom (I call my grandma "mom"), so tell me about how grandma (her mom) used to treat your wounds. Were you just as dare devilish as us and used to get hurt, too?

A: Actually, I was kind of a daredevil.

Q: Oh boy! What happened? What did you do?

A: I remember walking very far at least once a month, from where we used to live in Italy to go to the field where our land was to pick fruits and vegetables that we had planted. Other people from our town were there picking their crops as well. An hour into being in the field I took a rest, sat on a rock and drank some water. I noticed a beautiful fig tree across the field. You know I love figs! I walked over and without hesitation I climbed the tree like there was no tomorrow.

Q: Wait, wait, wait! Sorry to cut you off but you climbed the tree?! To steal someone's figs?! (I began to laugh so hard.)

A: Yes, they were ripe and ready to be eaten. But back to my story, I made sure no one was looking at me and I began climbing the tree. Now keep in mind, one fig I wanted so badly was about 7 feet up, so I kept climbing and climbing without looking down. I reached the fig and right when I went to grab it, I put my foot on a branch that had a thick thorn on it.

If I didn't want anyone to notice I was up there, they did now. I screamed at the top of my lungs! My mom came running to me and running after her came my dad and two of their friends. They got me down and tried to calm me down.

Q: How did they get the thorn out?

A: My mother had a handkerchief at her side and a pin attached to her bra. She rubbed the pin on her hair to sterilize it and started digging in my skin, making the hole a bit bigger

160

so I wouldn't feel the thorn as much when it came out.

Q: How was the needle sterile if grandma rubbed it on her hair?

A: Well, we didn't carry things like alcohol or peroxide when we left to go to the farm. So by rubbing it in her hair we kinda hoped, prayed, then believed it was cleaner than what it would have been coming off her bra.

Q: Gotcha! (I began to laugh again.) Now that I think of it, she always did carry a pin either on her bra or camisole. She got used to it, I guess. Was Grandma successful getting the thorn out?

A: Mamma mia!! Yes, and it hurt like a bitch! So much blood came out of my foot I thought I was going to die! I panicked and asked my mom to please make it stop! She screamed for my dad, "Gennaro! Gennaro vieni qua! Subito!" *[My great grandpa's name was Gennaro. She was telling him to come immediately.]*

My dad came and knew exactly what to do. He unzipped his pants and, you're gonna find this very strange, but he peed on my foot! It burned so bad but stopped most of the bleeding within 3 minutes.

My mom then used her handkerchief and wrapped up my foot, stuck it back in my shoe, let me rest for about 10 minutes, which felt like 10 seconds, and told me to get back to work. I looked at her in shock and she gave me a look that I took as "you shouldn't have been climbing that tree, you deserved what

161

happened to you, now get back to helping us pick so we can go home."

I trusted my parents' judgment. The hole in the bottom of my foot closed up by the time we got home and that was that.

Q: I bet you never climbed anyone's tree to steal figs again, right?

A: Climbed? No. Never again. But I did steal people's figs – only the ones I could reach, though.

In those days, far away from the hospital as they were, they needed a quick home remedy to stop the bleeding and prevent infection. Talk about sustainable medicine! Their "first aid kit" was just a pin and a handkerchief that Maria Grazia, my great grandma, always had tucked into her clothing, plus urine, an ancient renewable medicine that's always available.

⌘

PART SIX: ASIA

Everything at the Wrong Dose is Poison

Elizabeth Khololeyenko

KAZAKHSTAN, CENTRAL ASIA

Times have changed and society has evolved into a state of inefficiency where it's become difficult for life itself to flourish at a deeper level. Without realizing, our generation has come to know life in terms of materialism and social media. There's always food on the table, and our closets are bursting with clothes. We have gadgets for any difficulty that faces us. Our phones talk and tell us what to eat. Our main means of communication is over text. We have become materialistic, narcissistic, and inconsiderate of our fortunes and ignorant of how people used to value their assets and still do in other countries.

Looking back at life some few decades ago, we can see a great contrast in how people treated their resources. My mother grew up in Kazakhstan, Central Asia, and life was nearly opposite to what we experience now.

Kazakhstan for the most part was a working-class country; people worked to live and put food on the table. When asked about the overall living conditions she experienced as a child,

Irina, my mother replied, "...it's all that we knew." Clothes were passed on from anyone and everyone. Having a rip or a tear would not mean it is time to throw a sweater in the trash; it was sewed up and continued to serve its purpose until the fabric would ultimately give way. Style, when it came to dressing, was not a given like it is now to most of our society. Clothes were judged upon efficiency and comfort.

Shopping for clothes at a mall or a store was for people that had money and could ultimately be labeled rich. "I didn't even know what a mall looked like until I was about your age – there was no use for it," my mother admitted. The only stores that were visited were supermarkets and the local bazaar that sold everything from food to socks and books.

Nothing was disposable. My mother lived in the city, so her lifestyle was more or less modern. However, when school was out all the children were always sent to spend the summer at their summer house with their grandparents. It was very common not to find a single child living in the city when the weather got hot. Summer houses, my mother explained, were always medieval and used no technology at all besides a cord phone.

Food was grown in gardens bigger than the house itself – anything from strawberries, raspberries, peas to sea berries [sea buckthorn], *hurma* [persimmon], watermelon and sunflower seeds. Milk was delivered in a milk truck every now and then. All food was home made from scratch every day. There were no stores in sight for a good few miles, but some people would go out and post up on the road side to sell their vegetables and fruits for some income.

The house, as most, had no refrigerator but a root cellar. It used the earth's cool temperature instead of electricity. "The floor in one of the rooms would open up and there would be a ladder to descend with a flashlight," my mother explained laughing, remembering the struggle every summer. As for the heating aspect, they had a huge oven that was called a *pechka*. The closest description of it would be a brick oven . . . except it would not only be used for baking food but also to heat the whole house. It even had a warm, cozy space on top to sleep. These were a very durable system of heating and cooling and saved people lots of money.

PECHKA, BRICK OVEN FOR COOKING, HEATING, AND SLEEPING
(PHOTO © VODOLEJ / ADOBE STOCK)

Back in the city, neighborhoods mostly all looked the same. A few buildings to a playground, there were typically no private houses in these areas. Playgrounds consisted of a sandbox, swings and benches. Some were more modern and had a jungle gym. Kids would go out and play unsupervised from a very young age. It was a community with a milk man and a local grocer. The parents all knew each other and would automatically look out for the neighboring children playing. It was a trust that was understood and given. "Yes, it was that town where you can knock on someone's door and ask for a pinch of salt or sugar because you ran out while cooking," my mother joyfully explained. "Things were harder but simpler; people were closer to one another."

My mother's mother, my grandmother, used to work for a bakery almost all her life. This was considered a prestigious job in the sense that she had good access to bread and other food. "We would always have cookies," my mother boasted. "It wasn't a huge deal but it was still a luxury. People could not afford to always have baked goods from a bakery at the house unless they baked it themselves."

Living arrangements were usually connected families. My mother lived with her parents and the parents of her father. "It saved money and the grandparents would help out a lot with kids when the parents were at work," generally speaking. Every single commodity was valued and used to full advantage. People set things up to make life as efficient as possible.

A lot of jobs were at the local factories, stores, and food markets, which is another reason my grandmother's job was thought upscale. Those with more reputable office jobs would have to travel a little further into the city where such businesses were established.

Transportation wasn't an issue, at least for my grandfather, who had a motorcycle instead of a car. "It was a vintage motorcycle with a sidecar, of all things," my mother related, rolling her eyes. I guess this is where my grandfather spoiled himself. Not everyone could afford a car at the time or a motorcycle. The most common means of getting around for the general public was something called a tram. Trams were powered by electricity and ran on tracks but looked like buses with antennas. They are also called electric street railways, streetcars, or trolleys, and they still exist today, though they're probably not as common. Since it was a still an urban area, schools were zoned and not too far away from the place of residence. The lack of cars in the area gave space for beautiful parks full of trees and grassy areas, even in the city. "Now everything looks grey and dead, like it's been abandoned and nobody cares anymore."

Recycling was unheard of, and for a good reason: nothing was ever garbage. "Things like cookie tin, you will never find cookies in them, just a bunch of sewing equipment," my mother laughed. The only garbage was waste, from cooking or wrappers and such. Plastic bags were always reused until holes would appear. Unlike today, they weren't free with a purchase but actually had to be bought if you want to take your groceries home, unless you have your own, which is what most people did. People actually sold all types of plastic bags with different pictures and designs at the bazaar. Everything had value. Food was not allowed to go to waste. "Sometimes I sat for an hour at the table because I wasn't allowed to leave until I finished my portions," explains my mother. Now I know why she never throws away her own food. Knowing what's involved in the struggle gives people direction.

Toys were treasured and also passed along as children grew out of them. My mother owned a baby doll that she cherished. Her dad bought her an expensive doll for her birthday that was hard, shiny plastic and her mother bought the carriage to go along with it. "I was never happier in my entire life. I immediately ran outside to show off to the whole playground," she smiled.

Other typical toys were wooden blocks and rocking-horses. Unused household items would be handed to the children to play with; old pots, empty perfume bottles and all that sort of stuff made good knickknacks for kids' imaginations. "Everything could be a toy. It's just a matter of if you can think of what to do with things around the house. I used to flip a puffy stool upside down and rock on it pretending it was a ship."

I can't imagine children these days — with all the video games they play — spending their time thinking of stuff like that.

Free time wasn't spent going out to lunch and dinner. Restaurants and cafes were for special occasions only. As for fast food places, there were none! People spent their time ideally with family, watching shows on TV and playing board games. When my mother got older and well into her teenage years, there were no places to hang out. There were movie theater premiers here and there but besides that, only delinquents spent their time hanging on the streets. Her mother kept her busy with homework, chores, babysitting and piano lessons. "Every girl needs to know how to play the piano at the least," her mother would say.

People took pride in any type of knowledge because college wasn't a very common thing. However, even though her degree isn't valid in the United States, I am very proud to say that my mother earned a type of nursing degree a short while after finishing high school.

It's evident that we shouldn't deprive ourselves of all the great commodities that our time in history offers us. However, everything at the wrong dose is poison. All our pollution and excess waste is harming our health. Weather has never been so bi-polar, not even a decade ago. We are experiencing insane tides because of global warming, a much-underrated issue. Unlimited access to all ways of life is making us de-valorize materials and dispose of them in such a quick manner that nothing holds meaning anymore. Our social life is taking a toll because of our devaluation of communication. Children are dumbed down by technology and are overburdened with toys that they don't appreciate and that hold no meaning for them.

People always take the easy way out and have no care in the world because they don't know another world.... In the end, our lifestyle is linked to the wellbeing of everything and everybody.

⌘

Eat What's on Your Banana Leaf

Sanu Thomas

KERALA, INDIA

The world has changed so much in the last fifty years. The rate at which the consumer culture has grown in the past century is unprecedented. A small state in the southwest portion of India called Kerala was one of the few areas that remained untouched by the culture of consumerism, that is, until the last twenty-five years. A person that is familiar with the older ways in Kerala is Saramma, my mother.

The story begins in 1952, when Saramma was welcomed by a mother, father, two sisters, and three brothers. Three younger brothers arrived after her, bringing the household total to eleven members.

During my mother's childhood, almost everything inside the house was made by one of the family members. The utensils for serving the food were made usually from shells of old coconut. Most of the meals were served on cleaned banana leaves and were consumed using their hands. Everyone ate what was on their plate, or in this case, banana leaf, and nothing ever went to waste. They produced virtually no garbage. When cooking, if they came across some unwanted part of the vegetable or fish (like the bones), they just tossed it out the window and the animals and nature took care of it. There were never piles of garbage like you may see today; everything they used was essentially from the earth and as a result goes back to the earth. Plastic-based products were not part of their household at that time, and that also prevented the creation of garbage.

Things changed so much for my mother when she moved from one continent to another. Now she and I, a family of two, live in a three-bedroom home that has more space than the home she grew up in with a family of eleven. Though she has a closet full of sarees and other clothes, most of them are old, some over fifteen years. I believe this may have something to do with having grown up with very few clothes. She can't throw those old clothes out; she always finds another use for them. When I see a shirt with holes it goes in the garbage, but my mother will yell at me for throwing it away. First, she will try to fix it by sewing, but since I'm more modernized and can't be caught looking raggedy, she'll then turn it into a rag to wipe the floors or clean the house with.

No matter how much time has passed or where she lives, my mother still remains true to her humble beginnings. She's still the girl from Kerala who walks into our backyard garden with no shoes.

⌘

There Were Absolutely NO Commercials Addressing Depression, Over-active Bladder or Obesity

Michelle Coderias

KUDARAT, MINDANAO, PHILIPPINES

My grandmother, Filomena, was born in 1932 in Sultan Kudarat, a town in Mindanao, the second largest island and the largest agricultural area in the Philippines. Mindanao is about a 2-hour flight from the capital, Manila. Since she has immigrated to the United States, we have been very close.

My grandmother, noting the way that my sisters and I shop for clothes, said that people did not have so many clothes during her youth. Each item of clothing had more purpose, such as play clothes, work clothes or church clothes. The shoes that were worn for important functions were carved out of wood into intricate designs and painted. Also, many clothes were hand sewn. My grandmother was taught to become an expert seamstress so that she would be able to repair and also create instead of purchasing clothes.

GRANDMOTHER FILOMENA

In the Philippines, a girl's transition to womanhood is called her "debut," similar to a "sweet 16" or a "quinceañera." My grandmother recalls a beautiful dress she had wanted to wear but couldn't afford, so her own grandmother made a dress for her. It turned out very well made and even the detail of sewn-in sequins made it more beautiful than she had imagined.

Though a convenience store that they owned was their primary source of income, Filomena's family also owned and tended to a small farm – mostly root vegetables: taro, ginger, *ube* [purple yam], potatoes, etc. Her father had built a root cellar or an *ugat ng alak*, a dug-out area in the ground where it was cool and the sun could not get in, so vegetables could be stored for months.

Transportation in her town was mostly by foot or a cycle rickshaw (*ikot ng rickshaw*), a bike with a passenger attachment. Transporting people around town by cycle rickshaw would also be a form of income for families.

People didn't throw away leftover food. They either gave it to other people or to the animals. My grandmother laughs telling me about how she gave a fish bone to the dog, wondering if he would know how to eat it. But the dog expertly ate the fish head and all the meat in-between the bones. This to me seemed highly entertaining, considering my dog sniffs a piece of chicken and walks away with a "that's-not-good-enough-for-me" attitude.

GRANDMA'S STORE

One of the games my grandmother used to play was called *Palo-sebo*. It involved trying to climb a greased bamboo pole. This game is usually played during town fiestas, particularly in the provinces. The objective of the participants was to be the first person to reach the prize—a small bag—located at the top of the bamboo pole. The small bag usually contained money or toys. She remembers this game distinctly because during World War II, when she was 8 years old, the Japanese captured her town and she had to climb up a tree and hide for hours while the Japanese soldiers stormed into her aunt's house and murdered her aunt and her husband.

My grandmother and I are extremely close. I think since her immigration here to the United States her ideals and values have changed. In some ways she has engrossed herself into a lot of the "big American spending" that we all partake in. Part of that is also due to her extremely loving and generous personality; she tries to give whatever she has to people that she cares about. So, when we go out shopping, sometimes I have to be the one to remind her she's buying in excess. But I love her anyway, whether she is spending big or being frugal.

I visited the Philippines in 2005 when I was around the ripe age of 21 years old. My mother had blessed me with a new laptop, so I had this wonderful idea that I could document all the wonderful experiences of visiting my homeland as a "conscious" adult. It was a total culture shock. We visited in the wet season in July. It was incredibly hot.

My grandfather had passed away and I remember the funeral was completely different from our stifling American ones. The casket was in an open area and my uncle and aunts and their friends just hung around the body – played cards and got drunk every night. It was a much more relaxed environment. I liked it in a way. It made it seem more relatable to a death, like "hey we're sad to see you go, so we're just gonna pretend everything is normal and hang around you for a couple more days and celebrate your life."

I noticed there was less consumption and waste over there than we have in the US. They conserved bottles; when I bought soda in a glass bottle, they actually emptied it into a bag and we took the bag to go. Television commercials were about affordable food and medicine for your kids. There were absolutely NO commercials addressing depression, over-active bladder or obesity. I don't think anyone in the Philippines can afford medicine for issues like that.

⌘

Nothing My Generation Did Would Pollute the Environment

Lijuan Ye

CHINA

People are always busy. They may not have time to visit their parents or grandparents, but they have time to stay with Facebook for hours and hours. One sunny morning, I visited my grandparents. Although it's just a 20-minute walk, I realized that I hadn't visited them for months. We enjoyed a nice hot tea and had an interesting conversation about their past. They are about 70 years old and lived in a village in China until 1997. They said that since 1958 the communist system used labor vouchers. Everybody was equal; they needed to earn work points to exchange for products.

My grandparents planted enough vegetables and grain for the whole family and only exchanged labor points for basic needs they couldn't produce themselves, such as flavoring, meat, and cloth. To keep warm, they used quilts, and to cool off they used fans – a technology that's thousands of years old.

They didn't have to travel far because school and workplace were in or around the village. Grandma told me that in the 1960s, most people just walked or biked.

> Your grandpa is so skillful he can build a bicycle
> from components. We didn't have enough money
> to buy a bicycle, so we just bought the parts little
> by little.

Bicycle was the main means of transportation, and there were only a few cars in the city. Grandpa biked a few kilometers to the city for shopping, or sometimes 30 to 40 kilometers to a bigger market place. My grandpa is so strong that he could transport about 7200 kg grain [that might be an exaggeration] by bicycle at once.

My grandpa not only could make a bicycle, but he could fix it. There were no plastic bags – they wrapped their purchases in long dry grasses or paper, which they could just toss at the side of the road or burn in the kitchen.

I asked what they did in their leisure time, and Grandma said,

> Leisure time? What is leisure time? I was just
> doing all kinds of housework, when I didn't need
> to farm. The Chinese New Year is the leisure time
> in every year when everyone can get together and
> didn't need to work.

I asked them about climate change and the environment, and Grandpa said,

> In the past there were a lot of stars in the sky, and
> the elderly people could know the weather by the
> different locations of the stars. Now I see only a
> few stars in the sky of the city. We didn't think

about protecting the environment or worry about destroying it. We just got water from nature. Nothing my generation did would pollute the environment.

⌘

CONCLUSION

Skywoman seems to look me in the eye and ask, in return for this gift of a world on Turtle's back, what will I give in return?

- Robin Wall Kimmerer[1]

Sustainability, according to the United Nations, is a way to "meet the needs of the present without compromising the ability of future generations to meet their own needs."[2]

The survival of most populations depended on the sustainable practices incorporated into their culture. The Iroquois Confederacy enshrined the principle of sustainability in their Constitution, calling upon leaders to make decisions that would be good not only for the present but for future generations, up to the seventh generation.[3] Something similar to "seventh generation philosophy" has been retained among Ojibwa and many other indigenous cultures up to the present.[4]

We ourselves are the beneficiaries of more than seven previous generations of ancestors who preserved and handed down the world in which we live. There are handy lessons about sustainability to learn even from the recent ancestors of the previous two generations.

1. Though necessity dictated conservative use of resources and made excessive consumption impossible for most people of previous generations, even well-to-do people preferred not to over-spend or to throw things away.

2. People were aware that the whole community had to share and use the same resources such as water, and there were rules that everyone followed about preserving a healthy environment.

3. People were more connected to each other than to things

4. Energy sources were often renewable (wind, water) and the architecture and technology that people used emphasized energy efficiency.

PHOTO BY FRED MURPHY, 2010-08-02, BRUGES

Though the traditional way of life was more sustainable, it was not meeting the requirements of ever-increasing capitalist development, nor did it always satisfy people's longings for a more comfortable lifestyle. Mass production and mass consumption, which really took off after World War II, were based on the assumption of infinite resources. For example, in the U.S. and later many other parts of the world, highways and cars replaced rails, streetcars, trains, and trolleys. This enabled not only the growth of huge automobile and petrochemical industries, but also suburbanization, with millions of new single-family homes that each needed a car and a separate set of appliances.

This transition in the United States involved record-breaking government spending on the nation's highway system. The post-war boom set expectations high among Americans and to some extent people all over the world that growth could go on forever.

Today's so-called "cheap" products exhaust the earth's resources without compensating the community or the environment. That is, the manufacturers are able to set the price low because they "externalize" the cost of producing these commodities. And people buy these cheap products, throw them away, and buy more cheap products. As student Elizabeth Khololeyenko put it,

> People always take the easy way out and have no care in the world because they do not know another world.

GRASS ROOF ON HISTORIC HOUSE, PARK NEAR SOUTHAMPTON, UK

As climate change accelerates at rates beyond the expectations of many climate scientists, the need to change our ways is no longer optional. It is not enough for individuals to feel virtuous by sometimes following the mantra, "Reduce, reuse, recycle." Climate catastrophe looms, and in its wake follows social catastrophe. The new agenda may well be "Resilience, relinquishment, and restoration," a change in community lifestyle that Jem Bendell calls "deep adaptation."

> I hope the deep adaptation agenda of resilience, relinquishment and restoration can be a useful framework for community dialogue in the face of climate change. Resilience asks us "how do we keep what we really want to keep?" Relinquishment asks us "what do we need to let go of in order to not make matters worse?" Restoration asks us "what can we bring back to

help us with the coming difficulties and tragedies?"[5]

Knowing the experience of the older generations who grew up without feeling entitled to growth and abundance is eye-opening to the younger generation. It helps them understand that every "modern convenience" is not necessary, that some wasteful practices could indeed be relinquished in order to save our planet, safeguard its resources, and cherish the health of our environment. According to Eric Zencey,

> We need a new economic vision, an economics grounded on fundamental assumptions that are a better fit to reality, the reality of a finite planet.[6]

The Western economic system evolved and flourished based on the assumption that earth's resources are infinite. Rapid economic growth due to colonialism and later in the 1950s offered the appearance of infinite economic growth. We are gradually "discovering what it means to realize that our world is finite. But infinite-planet theories live on."[7]

There are fundamental questions that have to be answered soon. Do we want to live on a "factory planet" or a "garden planet"? Do we want the measure of our success to be "gross national product" or "gross national happiness"? Do we want a world where people think only of themselves or do we want healthy communities where people know they are all connected? How we decide will determine if we and our descendants will be able to survive and thrive.

Finally, we have to differentiate between our needs and wants. Pleasures and satisfactions are subjective. Wants are hierarchical, but needs are objective.

Robin Wall Kimmerer recommends that people in the rich countries learn from the worldview of indigenous people and "strive to become naturalized to place."

Being naturalized to place means to live as if this is the land that feeds you, as if these are the streams from which you drink, that build your body and fill your spirit. To become naturalized is to know that your ancestors lie in this ground. Here you will give your gifts and meet your responsibilities. To become naturalized is to live as if your children's future matters, to take care of the land as if our lives and the lives of all our relatives depend on it. Because they do.[8]

Supporting local farmers, farmers markets, and urban food markets are a start, but what are needed are more fundamental measures for safeguarding and replenishing the declining resource base. It will be important to transition to many more community-based and -run cooperatives and to take civil action to stop the big corporations from wanton exploitation of resources and unmitigated pollution.

There's a common belief that people "worked hard" in the "old days," while we have it easier today. In fact, because consumption beyond providing for "needs" was not the norm, the pressure to work constantly was absent for many of the elders interviewed for this project. The parents of both authors took summer family vacations out of town every year. Many shopkeepers in Iran closed their stores for several weeks each summer to spend time with family and relatives. Jonathan Ayoub, a student at College of Staten Island, explained how important summer vacations were to Americans of moderate means, and how they managed to pay for them. His mother told him that her parents, his grandparents, went away to "Camp Perry" every summer.

This was very typical of people in my time, especially the adults. They saved up for summer to go away on vacation and during the rest of the year they saved money and planned for the next summer getaway. My father knew how to make things work or cut corners and buy things that were not as popular but were on sale. For example, my father purchased me five pairs of jeans that were discounted due to faulty zippers that he got for a steal. Then he repaired the zippers himself.

These people were happy with what they had, that is, the basics. They did not need to work more to have more. As mentioned in the introduction, unleashed economic growth not only has undermined the sustainable use of planet resources, but has undermined communal life.

Despite all of that, the past sustainable ways of life have not totally disappeared and are beginning to reappear in small and large changes brought about by environmentalists around the world:

1. Recycling movements spreading throughout the world
2. Bicycle-friendly cities like Copenhagen and Amsterdam in Europe and Minneapolis and Seattle in the U.S.; rental bicycles in New York and other cities
3. Garage sales
4. Compost
5. Farmers markets
6. Second hand stores
7. Emergence of communal housing
8. The "tiny house" fad, building sustainable small houses
9. Using tote bags for shopping
10. Measures to reduce exposure to second-hand smoke
11. The popular opposition to fossil fuels and pipelines
12. The push for solar and wind energy
13. The international agroecology movement

As these movements gain momentum and spread, it could lead to less consumption, less use of fossil fuel, and more attention to the environmental costs of various products.

If peasants and farmers increasingly convert to ecological farming methods that preserve the soil and also shift their focus to providing the needs of the community rather than international trade, local food security will increase. There could be many political implications. With minimal use of non-renewable energy and with the restoration of national and regional food security, people would not see any reason for competition – up to and including war – among the great powers for external natural resources.

The environmental movement, if successful, will help people stop worrying about Armageddon and the imminent end of the world and will give them a reason to have faith in the future again.

---

[1] Robin Wall Kimmerer, Braiding Sweetgrass: Indigenous Wisdom, Scientific Knowledge, and the Teachings of Plants, Minneapolis, MN: Milkweed Editions, 2013, p. 8.

[2] Eric Zencey, The Other Road to Serfdom and the Path to Sustainable Democracy, January 1, 2012, UPNE Publisher.

[3] An Iroquois Perspective. In Vecsey C, Venables RW, editors, *American Indian Environments: Ecological Issues in Native American History*, New York: Syracuse University Press, 1980, pp. 173f. See also https://nativeinsight.blogspot.com/2012/11/seventh-generation.html.

[4] Patty Loew, *Seventh Generation Earth Ethics: Native Voices of Wisconsin*. Wisconsin Historical Society Press; 1 edition (September 8, 2014)

[5] Jem Bendell, Deep Adaptation: A Map for Navigating Climate Tragedy, IFLAS Occasional Paper 2, www.iflas.info, July 27th, 2018. http://www.lifeworth.com/deepadaptation.pdf

[6] Zencey, p. xvii

[7] Zencey, p. xviii

[8] Kimmerer, pp. 214f.

APPENDIX

Some Considerations about the Environment and Sustainability

By Davoud Tehrani

All over the world one sees an extraordinary environmental movement. It's happening on both the micro and macro levels. Individuals are taking actions such as switching from cars to bicycles, walking, or public transportation for commuting; recycling; composting; and seeking out organic food and even clothing.

Besides individuals, increasing numbers of non-governmental organizations (NGOs) are devoted to environmental issues, and to some extent government agencies and even private enterprises are taking action. The UN holds conferences on renewable energy and enlists a majority of nations in climate agreements. The UN Food and Agriculture Organization (FAO) has adopted the term "agroecology."

These are signs of a growing realization that we are nearing our limits and cannot forever continue to use up non-renewable resources while destroying the habitat of our species by piling up waste and polluting the land and water that support human life.

Nevertheless, we have a way to go if we want to preserve a home for our species. The problem is too big to be remedied by individual actions alone.[1]

Sustainable habits and even the concept of sustainability have not yet become everyday parts of our culture, and most big corporations are doing their best to overlook the grim realities. Mass production and its enabler, mass consumption, continue as a malaise of modern times. Under the current dominant economic model, the purpose of production is not to provide for human needs but to guarantee ever-increasing profit. Rarely do we hear anyone question the need for continuous growth of the Gross Domestic Product (GDP), a measure of all the economic activity that involves money. The result is that humanity has to contend with an uncontrollable machine that creates both massive waste and products that are themselves harmful to nature and to human communities. It is as if the largest companies and the governments that protect them are in a race, no longer under human control, to exhaust global resources and fill all possible spaces – land, sea, and air – with garbage before their rivals can do so.

Economists say that the costs of production are being "externalized" onto the community and the environment. This means that manufacturers do not pay the true cost of the products they manufacture and thus are able to sell commodities – including hugely wasteful piles of unneeded commodities – at artificially low prices, thus stimulating over-consumption on the part of the population.

How does that work? Companies "externalize" much of the cost of research and development onto the community by taking advantage of tax breaks, government loans and grants, and publicly supported research (e.g., at universities and other institutions). Manufacturers also "externalize" a portion of the costs of production onto both the community and the environment. For example, they do not pay for cleaning up their pollution, for depleting natural resources, for disposing of their wastes or for the eventual disposal of the commodities and packaging they produce. The community and the environment bear those costs. The manufacturers create unhealthy conditions by sending toxins into the environment, and the population and medical system bear the costs. Manufacturers degrade the water, air, topsoil, and other aspects of the environment but do not pay the costs of restoring them. By "externalizing" the costs of production, manufacturers can sell commodities at artificially low prices that do not represent the true costs of making these commodities. These "cheap" products then are bought, thrown away, and replaced by new purchases in a cycle of endless over-consumption that in turn keeps the mass production machine over-producing. This is why the pace of environmental destruction and degradation seems to be increasing.

In the recent past in most parts of the world, consumerism was not part of the culture. Consumption was not tied to social status. Most people, both poor and more prosperous, owned only a few pairs of shoes and sets of clothing, and these could be repaired many times over regardless of the wearers' social class in the community. Even just a few decades ago, people walked much more than they do today and used bicycles and public transportation like streetcars and trolleys.

STREETCAR, ROME, ITALY

Things were not cheap and people valued them. Prices of things were closer to the actual cost of producing them, and people expected them to be durable. There was a general ethic of appreciating the value of things, whether they were made at home or purchased. Wasting things or money seemed wrong to people. In many areas, people used renewable energy and methods for cooling and heating.

It is true that many people in the past did not have a choice in the way they lived and would have preferred more comforts. But we at this moment are all in the same boat with few apparent choices about how to live in a way that doesn't cause the boat to sink.

In the past, production and consumption were primarily organized around the satisfaction of human needs. In modern times, the requirements of the market have replaced human necessities as the purpose of production and consumption.

It is hard to choose a lifestyle that does not pollute and exhaust the environment. Some of us have settled into a comfort zone where we hardly ever think of how the environment is affected by our actions. For example, we rarely think of the environmental effects of driving a short distance instead of walking or of regularly eating foods that have to be flown from the other side of the world. We no longer distinguish between our needs and our wants. Today, however, we have reached a time where people are seeing the need to take more responsibility for the effects of our lifestyles.

Stories of the past give us some creative ideas on how to live more sustainably. We could do away with plastic bags and bottles, try to fix things, create less garbage or no garbage at all, resist consuming merely for immediate gratification of our wants, build community, live simply, and take the attitude that small is beautiful. It was the old way of life that inspired the minimalist movement, including tiny houses, communities with sustainable weather-proof housing, car-sharing, urban farming, etc.

If in the "old days" people could not consume more because of limited family resources, today we have to control how much we consume because the earth itself is limited. There are limits to nonrenewable energy, rare metals, potable water, and the capacity of the environment to safely absorb the waste and pollution associated with mass production. With the rate we are consuming now, it would not be surprising if future generations had to go back to using public kitchens and pubic baths and would have to get around on foot and by bicycle.

Abundance in one part of the world alone can last forever. Yet the global environment would quickly collapse were the rest of the world to attempt to consume at the level of the rich countries.

Tehran, the capital of Iran, is so polluted and has so many cars in the streets that walking is no longer a pleasant experience and it's too dangerous to bike even if some people want to do so. On the other hand, owning a car is no longer a matter of prestige, as it once was, but a requirement because the city lacks a network of fast public transportation.

The culture of consumerism has become so enmeshed in our lives that it seems there is only one way to live. If your shirt or pants get old or have a rip, if you get tired of your shoes, if an appliance needs repair, if a pen needs ink, just throw them away and buy new ones. If your car is causing problems, sell it and purchase a new one. The discarding solution comes to mind by habit and automatically. This is what it is called a "throwaway culture." Of course, "cheap" products enable this habit.

Products are only "cheap," though, because the cost of damaging the environment has never been calculated into their cost. Those free plastic shopping bags (often doubled by the clerks) or plastic water bottles cost nature many times over the cost of the food and water we buy in them. In fact, their cost is irreversible harm to nature, because nature cannot process, digest, and absorb plastic. Plastics are not biodegradable. Or consider inexpensive clothing and shoes made of synthetic materials, throwaway plastic plates and decorations, etc. These "cheap" products cost nature so dearly that if they were priced at their real cost to the environment, nobody could afford them.

The people living on earth at this moment are faced with urgent questions:

1. Since we cannot totally go back to the traditional way of life in order to once again generate a balance between human needs and available resources in nature, how can we manage to create a <u>new</u> sustainable way of life?

2. How can we stop externalizing the costs of human and social development to the detriment of nature?

3. How can we live a healthy life without damaging our planet or borrowing resources from future generations?

Theoretical approach

The scientific study of environmental degradation, deforestation, and even climate change became important starting in the late 18th century, according to sociologist John Bellamy Foster.[2] Natural scientists including Matthias Jakob Schleiden, Carl Fraas, Charles Lyell and Charles Darwin analyzed the destructive effects of wide scale agriculture and other activities. Schleiden criticized those who "squander" plant life out of the "selfish pursuit of profit," saying they operated according to the "moral Vileness" expressed in the phrase "après nous le déluge."[3]

In 1839, writing about his famous journey on the Beagle, Charles Darwin attributed the almost complete deforestation of the isolated South Atlantic island of St. Helena to the goats introduced by European settlers starting in 1502.[4]

The growing scientific concern about the destruction of the natural environment influenced Karl Marx and Friedrich Engels, who studied the works of Fraas, Schleiden, and others as they developed their own ideas:

> The first effect of cultivation is useful, but finally devastating through deforestation, etc.... The

conclusion is that cultivation—when it proceeds in natural growth and is not *consciously controlled* (as a bourgeois he [Fraas] naturally does not reach this point)—leaves deserts behind it.[5]

In *Capital*, Marx argued that the process of capital accumulation was recklessly destroying the human and environmental foundations of life.[6]

Economic growth and the environment

In *Enough is Enough,* Rob Dietz outlines the unprecedented environmental problems that have been mounting over the last hundred years: a destabilized global climate, widespread poverty, deforestation, soil erosion, pollution of waters, and the species extinction crisis.[7]

People today are living by the mantra "the more the better": big houses, expensive cars, vast collections of clothing, etc. Though mass production and mass consumption provide cheap commodities to everyone alike, the never-ending growth in production disregards the fact that there is a limit to the earth's resources. Cheap merchandise does not last; it ends up in the trash before long. Can we slow down the economy while the standard conviction is that economic growth is desirable? It is for this reason that Robert Dietz talks about "the destination of enough" – which he defines as an economy that "cares for both people and the planet." Instead of economic growth, an economy devoted to the needs of capital, we need the "steady-state economy."[8] Dietz is associated with the Center for the Advancement of the Steady State Economy (CASSE), whose mission is to show that continuous economic growth is environmentally unfeasible and undesirable.[9]

In general, "the dominant economic philosophy of modernity has been and is more—more people, more production, more money, and more consumption," says Dietz. Yet people are only beginning to realize that this process does not endlessly improve people's lives and it leads to catastrophe as we surpass ecological limits.[10]

The modern manufacturing economy rests on extracting natural resources and transforming them to unnatural substances that remain exterior to the environment. The more the economy expands, the more resources it uses and the more waste it produces. Can we continue this trend and close our eyes to the reality that the planet is finite?[11]

Before the industrial revolution, a relatively small space in the biosphere was occupied by human production, consumption, and waste. However, this is no longer true. Due to the exponential growth of human population and especially human production, we are overtaking the ability of the biosphere to support us. Between 1900 and 2008 the world population grew four-fold, from 1.5 billion to 6.8 billion people. Over the same period, the world GDP increased 25-fold, from $2 trillion to $51 trillion (corrected for inflation).[12]

The global economy has become so large that it is endangering the natural resources and processes that make human life possible. Ecological realities put a limit on economic growth. We cannot forever cut trees at a rate faster than they grow back and release more carbon dioxide than the oceans, forests, and soils can absorb. We are now in a situation of "ecological overshoot," consuming resources and producing waste beyond the capacity of global ecosystems to sustain.[13] This was the message to investors in the 2011 annual report of Portfolio 21, a global mutual fund:

> Although the news media continue to focus on the upheaval and volatility of financial markets..., ecological limits to economic growth is the real

story of the century. Environmental disasters have been intensifying as economic growth struggles against natural and man-made limits.[14]

While some aspects of new technology (medicines, electricity, communication) and mass production (wide availability of useful products at reasonable costs) may be beneficial, other aspects are harmful (weapons of mass destruction). And continued economic growth at the pace to which we've become accustomed comes at too great a cost to the environment.

Price vs True Cost

Are "free" plastic bags, plastic spoons and forks, paper and cardboard actually free? How much are they costing our planet? What is the real cost (value) of these "free" products? Where do these entirely free things come from and, more importantly, where do they end up?

Waste is generally not included when calculating the price of commodities. Neither the value of the nonrenewable resources that are consumed in making these products, nor the cost of disposing of the waste, nor the negative effects of the pollution on the environment and human health are calculated when "cheap" commodities are priced. If these factors were included in the price, no one could afford to put his or her groceries in a plastic bag.

LANDFILL, DELAWARE COUNTY, NY

Plastic bags are synthetic materials made of polyethylene, also known as polythene. These materials are hazardous to manufacture and take up to 1,000 years to degrade. Plastic breaks down to smaller and smaller toxic pieces that pollute the water and the soil and end up in the stomachs and tissues of animals and even human beings.

Plastic bags are a relatively recent invention that were not used in grocery stores until the 1980s. But today, between 500 billion and 1 trillion single-use plastic bags are put into circulation every year worldwide, or up to 2 million a minute. The results have been so alarming – toxic smoke from burning rubbish containing discarded bags, flooding caused by clogged drains and sewage systems, deaths of cows and sheep from eating plastic, and especially the deaths of more than 1 million marine animals per year – that many cities and even countries have instituted bans or taxes on plastic bags. The petroleum and plastics industries strongly oppose such regulations.[15, 16]

One of the cities that banned plastic bags is San Francisco. In 2007, arguing for the need for such a ban, Jared Blumenfeld, director of San Francisco's Department of the Environment, reported that only 1% of plastic bags had been recycled in the previous 10 years, and that, unlike aluminum cans, plastic bags cannot be profitably recycled.[17]

It is not just plastic bags, of course.

> As of 2015, more than 6.9 billion tons of plastic waste had been generated. Around 9 percent of that was recycled, 12 percent was incinerated, and 79 percent accumulated in landfills or environment.[18]

It's only gotten worse since 2015. In the summer of 2019, the authors were throwing their own waste plastics into the large container for glass, plastic, cans, and recyclables at the Delaware County landfill in the Catskills region of New York. An employee approached and starting tossing everything into the container for garbage, saying, in effect, "we can't recycle these anymore."

What happened? Starting in 1992, much of the plastic waste in the U.S. was sent to China for cheap recycling, but that ended in 2018, when China "banned imports of dirty foreign garbage."[19] One of the problems had been that U.S. cities were allowing consumers to mix all sorts of things together in the recycling bins and were not spending the money to sort it properly. When China quit paying for this dirty mix, the U.S. was faced with the reality that recycling and cleaning up the environment might be a cost, not an income opportunity. For example, Stamford, Connecticut, earned $95,000 from its recyclables in 2017, but in 2018 it had to spend $700,000 to dispose of recyclables.[20] This then raises the question of whether such toxic items ought to be manufactured in the first place.

One of the most visible and distressing results of the unlimited production and consumption of plastic commodities is that beaches worldwide are littered with plastic bottles, plastic straws, plastic bags, and other plastic fragments, both on top of and under the sand. In fact, 73% of the world's beach litter is plastic. Even uninhabited Henderson Island in the middle of the Pacific is affected.[21]

In December 2018, news outlets reported a sad and shocking discovery. A dead whale was found washed ashore on a beach in eastern Indonesia with 13 pounds of plastic in its stomach: 115 plastic cups, four plastic bottles, 25 plastic bags, a nylon sack, and 1,000 other items. The cause of death could not be determined for sure, but the finding gave a hint of the dangers of plastic waste to even the largest of living creatures in the seas.[22]

Economic growth and poverty

Mainstream economists say that Gross Domestic Product (GDP) and economic growth translate to wellbeing. The public is told to accept environmental degradation as the inevitable, and acceptable, cost of a higher standard of living for all. However, recent economic growth has not lived up to that promise. According to a 2006 United Nations report,

Despite the twenty-five-fold increase in the size of the global economy over the past century, more than 1 billion people still live on less than $1 per day, and a total of 2.7 billion live on less than $2 per day.[23]

Because the world system operates under capitalist principles and laws, the benefits of economic growth have been very unevenly distributed. A miniscule share of the economic growth actually goes to the world's poor. Only 60 cents out of every \$100 in the world's economic growth in the last decade of the 20th century went to those living on less than \$1 a day.[24] The lion's share goes to a tiny minority. In terms of income alone, not including holdings in wealth,

> [T]he richest 10 percent of Americans are now taking more than half of the economic pie, while the top 1 percent is taking more than one fifth.[25]

The inequality is even more extreme in terms of wealth. In 2015, the world's richest 62 people, a number so small they could all fit on a city bus, owned more wealth than half the population of the whole world together.[26] Two years later, three individuals – Jeff Bezos, Bill Gates, and Warren Buffett – in the United States together owned more wealth than the bottom 50% of the American public. Meanwhile, one out of every five American households (a higher proportion among people of color) are "underwater," that is, "have zero or negative net worth to fall back on."[27]

Not everyone is experiencing the negative aspects of unlimited economic growth. Across the globe, in both rich and poor countries, a portion of the population have gained benefits from some aspects of economic growth even while the gap between the super-rich and everyone else has been widening. In every country there are people who have increased their disposable (cash) income and improved their standard of living in terms of housing, sanitation, education, modern means of communication, medical care, and access to cheap commodities (including cheap food).

During the same period of economic growth when the wealth of a small elite has ballooned, globalization has involved job loss and disruption of the lives of millions of workers.[28]

According to the U.S. Bureau of Labor Statistics, two out of every five displaced manufacturing workers who were rehired in 2016 experienced a wage reduction. One out of every four displaced manufacturing workers took a pay cut of greater than 20 percent.[29] For the average worker earning the median manufacturing wage of $39,500 per year, this meant an annual loss of at least $7,900.

Many displaced workers in the manufacturing sector had to shift over to lower paid service sectors. For example, between 1993 and 2017, the manufacturing sector lost about 4.5 million jobs. At the same time, the leisure and hospitality sector gained 5.4 million jobs, which has an average wage of $13 an hour, almost half that of the average wage in the manufacturing sector.[30]

Even the economic benefits to the relatively lucky ones may be actually offset by declining real income, resulting in a net loss. In the U.S., according to Public Citizen's Global Trade Watch,[31]

> The Center for Economic and Policy Research discovered that when comparing the lower prices of cheaper goods to the income lost from low-wage competition under current trade policy, the trade-related wage losses outweigh the gains in cheaper goods for the vast majority of U.S. workers. [32] U.S. workers without college degrees (58 percent of the workforce) have likely lost an amount equal to 12.2 percent of their wages under NAFTA-style trade even after accounting for the benefits of cheaper goods.[33] That means a net loss of more than $3,965 per year for a worker earning the median annual wage of $32,500.[34]

Indeed, the massive economic growth has come at a very high cost to the environment and to human beings. Tropical tree cover loss (removal of tree canopy from human or natural causes) was 15.8 million hectares (39.0 million acres) in 2017, the worst year on record.[35] Sources of freshwater in many parts of the world are being used up faster than they can be refilled. In fact, warns a NASA water scientist, "the water table is dropping all over the world. There's not an infinite supply of water."[36] Due to unsustainable agricultural methods and erosion, topsoil, which is necessary for growing food, is being degraded and lost 10 to 40 times faster than it can be naturally restored.[37]

There is no sign that human suffering will decline rather than increase if we continue on this path. In addition to a widespread increase in debt and economic insecurity at all but the highest income levels, unchecked economic growth has resulted in devastation at the level of the most vulnerable people. Countless human beings have been dispossessed of their land and livelihoods and plunged into abysmal poverty. Millions of people have become refugees from wars over resources and there is a growing mass of climate refugees fleeing drought and floods. A 2009 report from the Environmental Justice Foundation warned of up to 150 million climate refugees by 2050.[38]

In sum, we are allowing the planet on which we all depend to be destroyed for the sake of unlimited economic growth that does not even benefit the majority of humanity. We are, so to speak, eating our seed corn, cashing in our insurance policies, and fouling our own nest. We are acting like Esau in the Bible, who sold his birthright for a bowl of porridge. Is this truly the only way to live?

[1] Matt Wilkins, More recycling won't solve plastic pollution: It's a lie that wasteful consumers cause the problem and that changing our individual habits can fix it. *Scientific American*, July 6, 2018. https://blogs.scientificamerican.com/observations/more-recycling-wont-solve-plastic-pollution/

[2] John Bellamy Foster, Capitalism and the accumulation of catastrophe. *Monthly Review*, Vol 63, Issue 07, Dec. 1, 2011.

[3] M.J. Schleiden, *The Plant: A Biography* (London: H. Baillere, 1853), 295, 303–7. Quoted in John Bellamy Foster, Capitalism and the Accumulation of Catastrophe. *Monthly Review*, Vol 63, Issue 07, Dec. 1, 2011. The phrase is attributed to Louis XV and/or his mistress, Madame de Pompadour, in reference to the coming French Revolution.

[4] Ibid.

[5] Karl Marx and Frederick Engels, *Collected Works*, vol. 42 (New York: International Publishers, 1975), 558–59. Quoted in John Bellamy Foster, 2011.

[6] Karl Marx, *Capital*, vol. 1 (London: Penguin, 1976), p. 381. Quoted in John Bellamy Foster, 2011, who notes Marx's debt to Schleiden.

[7] Rob Dietz and Dan O'Neil. *Enough is Enough: Building a Sustainable Economy in a World of Finite Resources*. Berrett-Koehler Pub. Inc., San Francisco, CA, 2013), pp. 4ff.

[8] Ibid, p. 8. The expression is Herman Daly's.

[9] Ibid, p. 9

[10] Ibid, pp. 15f

[11] Ibid. p. 17

[12] Ibid

[13] Ibid, 21

[14]- Leslie Christian and Carsten Henningsen, Portfolio 21 annual Report, June 30, 2011. Quoted in Dietz, 2013, p. 25.

[15] Douglas Lober, Plastic bags usage + bans around the world, Reusethisbag.com.

[16] Sharon Lerner, Waste only: How the plastics industry is fighting to keep polluting the world, *The Intercept,* July 20, 2019.

[17] Ben Arnoldy, Seldom recycled, plastic grocery bags face bans in S.F., *The Christian Science Monitor,* March 29, 2007.

[18] *National Geographic*, Planet or plastic? 10 shocking facts about plastic. 2018.

[19] Edward Humes, You can't recycle garbage. *Sierra,* July/Aug. 2019.

[20] Ibid.

[21] *National Geographic*, Planet or plastic? What happens to the plastic we throw out? The journey of plastic around the globe. 2018.

[22] *Vision Times*, Dead whale found with 115 plastic cups in stomach, Dec. 5, 2018.

[23]- United Nations Millennium Project, "Fast Facts: The Faces of Poverty" (United Nations Millennium Project, UN Development Group, 2006). Quoted in Dietz, p. 27.

[24] David Woodward and Andrew Simms, *Growth Isn't Working: The Unbalanced Distribution of Benefits and Costs from Economic Growth.* London: New Economics Foundation, 2006. Quoted in Dietz, p. 27.

[25] Public Citizen's Global Trade Watch, NAFTA's Legacy: Lost Jobs, Lower Wages, Increased Inequality, February 2018.

[26] Deborah Hardoon, Ricardo Fuentes-Nieva, and Sophia RicardoAyele, An Economy For the 1%: How privilege and power in the economy drive extreme inequality and how this can be stopped, Oxfam briefing paper, 18 Jan 2016.

[27] Chuck Collins and Josh Hoxie, Billionaire bonanza: the Forbes 400 and the rest of us, Institute for Policy Studies, Nov. 2107.

[28] Public Citizen's Global Trade Watch, op. cit.

[29] U.S. Bureau of Labor Statistics, "Displaced Workers Summary," U.S. Department of Labor, Aug. 25, 2016.

[30] U.S. Bureau of Labor Statistics, "Industries by Supersector and NAICS Code," U.S. Department of Labor, accessed Feb. 8, 2018.

[31] Public Citizen's Global Trade Watch, op. cit.

[32] Dean Baker and Mark Weisbrot, "Will New Trade Gains Make Us Rich?" Center for Economic and Policy Research (CEPR) Paper, Oct. 2001.

[33] U.S. Census Bureau, "Educational Attainment in the United States: Table 2. Educational Attainment of the Population 25 Years and Over, by Selected Characteristics: 2017," accessed Feb. 12, 2018, for the share of workforce without a college degree. Cited in Baker and Weisbrot, 2001.

[34] Social Security Administration, "Wage Statistics for 2016," accessed Feb. 12, 2018, for median wage information. Cited in Baker and Weisbrot, 2001.

[35] Mikaela Weisse and Liz Goldman, 2017 was the second-worst year on record for tropical tree cover loss, Global Forest Watch, June 27, 2018.

[36] Tim Smedley, Is the world running out of fresh water? Future Now, BBC, April 12, 2017.

[37] World Economic Forum interview with John Crawford (Univ. of Sydney), What if the world's soil runs out? *TIME*, Dec. 14, 2012.

[38] John Vidal, Global warming could create 150 million 'climate refugees' by 2050, *The Guardian*, Nov. 2, 2009.

BIBLIOGRAPHY

Arnoldy, Ben, Seldom recycled, plastic grocery bags face bans in S.F., *The Christian Science Monitor. March 29, 2007.*
https://www.csmonitor.com/2007/0329/p01s03-ussc.html

Baker, Dean and Weisbrot, Mark, Will new trade gains make us rich? Center for Economic and Policy Research (CEPR) Paper, Oct. 2001.
http://www.cepr.net/documents/publications/trade_2001_10_03.pdf.

Bendell, Jem, Deep Adaptation: A Map for Navigating Climate Tragedy, IFLAS Occasional Paper 2, www.iflas.info, July 27th, 2018.
http://www.lifeworth.com/deepadaptation.pdf

Foster, John Bellamy, Capitalism and the Accumulation of Catastrophe. *Monthly Review*, Vol 63, Issue 07, Dec. 1, 2011.
https://monthlyreview.org/2011/12/01/capitalism-and-the-accumulation-of-catastrophe/

Christian, Leslie and Henningsen, Carsten, Portfolio 21 annual Report, June 30, 2011.

Collins, Chuck and Hoxie, Josh, Billionaire bonanza: the Forbes 400 and the rest of us, Institute for Policy Studies, Nov. 2107.
https://inequality.org/wp-content/uploads/2017/11/BILLIONAIRE-BONANZA-2017-Embargoed.pdf

Crawford, John, (interview). World Economic Forum, (Univ. of Sydney), What if the world's soil runs out? TIME, Dec. 14, 2012.
http://world.time.com/2012/12/14/what-if-the-worlds-soil-runs-out/

Dietz, Rob and O'Neil, Dan. *Enough is Enough: Building a Sustainable Economy in a World of Finite Resources.* Berrett-Koehler Pub. Inc., San Francisco, CA, 2013.

Hardoon, Debrah, Ricardo Fuentes-Nieva, and Sophia RicardoAyele, An Economy For the 1%: How privilege and power in the economy drive extreme inequality and how this can be stopped, Oxfam briefing paper, 18 Jan 2016.
https://oxfamilibrary.openrepository.com/bitstream/handle/10546/592 643/bp210-economy-one-percent-tax-havens-180116-en.pdf;jsessionid=5550CBE114D22C3D7A5F01E1024CB7F9?sequence= 47

Kille, Leighton Walter and Rachael Stephens, Plastics, human health and environmental impacts: the road ahead. *Journalist's Resource*, Shorenstein Center on Media, Politics and Public Policy, Harvard Kennedy School, Oct 9, 2014.
https://journalistsresource.org/studies/environment/pollution-environment/plastics-environmental-health-literature-review

Kimmerer, Robin Wall, *Braiding Sweetgrass: Indigenous Wisdom, Scientific Knowledge, and the Teachings of Plants*, Minneapolis, MN: Milkweed Editions, 2013.

Lober, Douglas, Plastic bags usage + bans around the world, Reusethisbag.com. March 27th, 2018.
https://www.reusethisbag.com/articles/plastic-bag-bans-worldwide/

Loew, Patty, *Seventh Generation Earth Ethics: Native Voices of Wisconsin*. Wisconsin Historical Society Press; 1 edition (September 8, 2014).

Marx, Karl and Engels, Frederick, *Collected Works,* vol. 42 (New York: International Publishers, 1975).

Marx, Karl. *Capital*, vol. 1 (London: Penguin, 1976).

National Geographic, 10 shocking facts about plastic.
https://www.nationalgeographic.com/environment/plastic-facts/

National Geographic, Planet or plastic? What happens to the plastic we throw out.
https://www.nationalgeographic.com/magazine/2018/06/the-journey-of-plastic-around-the-globe/

Paul, Heike. *The Myths That Made America: An Introduction to American Studies*. Bielefeld: Transcript Verlag, 2014 (open access). http://www.jstor.org/stable/j.ctv1wxsdq

Public Citizen's Global Trade Watch, NAFTA's Legacy: Lost Jobs, Lower Wages, Increased Inequality. https://www.citizen.org/sites/default/files/nafta_factsheet_deficit_jobs_wages_feb_2018_final.pdf

Schleiden, M.J. *The Plant: A Biography* (London: H. Baillere, 1853).

Smedley, Tim, Is the world running out of fresh water? Future Now, BBC, April 12, 2017. http://www.bbc.com/future/story/20170412-is-the-world-running-out-of-fresh-water

United Nations Millennium Project, Fast Facts: The Faces of Poverty, UN Development Group, 2006.

Vecsey, Christopher and Robert W. Venables, *American Indian Environments: Ecological Issues in Native American History,* Syracuse University Press, New York, 1980.

Vidal, John, Global warming could create 150 million 'climate refugees' by 2050, *The Guardian*, Nov. 2, 2009. https://www.theguardian.com/environment/2009/nov/03/global-warming-climate-refugees

Vision Times, Dead whale found with 115 plastic cups in stomach, Dec. 5, 2018. http://www.visiontimes.com/2018/12/05/dead-whale-found-with-115-plastic-cups-in-stomach.html

Weisse, Mikaela and Liz Goldman, 2017 was the second-worst year on record for tropical tree cover loss, Global Forest Watch, June 27, 2018. https://blog.globalforestwatch.org/data/2017-was-the-second-worst-year-on-record-for-tropical-tree-cover-loss

Wilkins Matt, More recycling won't solve plastic pollution: It's a lie that wasteful consumers cause the problem and that changing our individual habits can fix it. *Scientific American*, July 6, 2018. https://blogs.scientificamerican.com/observations/more-recycling-wont-solve-plastic-pollution/

Woodward, David and Andrew Simms, *Growth Isn't Working: The Unbalanced Distribution of Benefits and Costs from Economic Growth*. London: New Economics Foundation, 2006. Quoted in Dietz, p. 27.

Zency Eric, *The Other Road to Serfdom and the Path to Sustainable Democracy*, January 1, 2012, UPNE Publisher.

ABOUT THE EDITORS

Davoud Tehrani, PhD, is a writer and sociologist. Before earning his PhD in sociology from the Graduate Center of the City University of New York, he received a B.S. in horticulture from the University of Ahwaz, Iran. Dr. Tehrani has written numerous fiction and non-fiction books and articles in Persian, including *Figurine, Negative Aspects of Punishment, Angel of Hell* and most recently, *The Story of Human Sciences*. Besides writing and gardening, Dr. Tehrani enjoys teaching sociology, formerly at the College of Staten Island and currently at Westchester Community College.

Ruth Wangerin, PhD, MPH, is an anthropologist and retired public health educator. Besides previous public health work related to tuberculosis and smoking, her research and writing has been on religious movements, chemical warfare, labor, and agroecology. *The Children of God: A Make-Believe Revolution?* told the story of youth looking for purpose and a new way of life. Recent articles include "The academic caste system" and "The adjunct professor as chimera." Although her favorite bumper sticker reads, "I'd rather be gardening," Dr. Wangerin finds meaning in teaching anthropology and getting to know today's youth. She has been at the College of Staten Island and now teaches at Westchester Community College and Lehman College.